Paper *Fold It*

D0124600

STEVE & MEGUMI BIDDLE

D&C
David and Charles

A DAVID & CHARLES BOOK
Copyright © David & Charles Limited 2008

David & Charles is an F+W Publications Inc. company
4700 East Galbraith Road
Cincinnati, OH 45236

First published in the UK in 2008

Text Copyright © Steve and Megumi Biddle
Illustrations Copyright © Megumi Biddle
Origami Design Folds Copyright © Steve and Megumi Biddle
Photographs Copyright © David and Charles 2008

A catalogue record for this book is available from the British Library.

ISBN-13: 978-0-7153-2586-5 hardback
ISBN-10: 0-7153-2586-8 hardback
ISBN-13: 978-0-7153-2585-8 paperback
ISBN-10: 0-7153-2585-X paperback

Printed in China by SNP Leefung Pte Ltd
for David & Charles
Brunel House   Newton Abbot   Devon

Executive Editor Cheryl Brown
Desk Editor Bethany Dymond
Project Editor Ame Verso
Senior Designer Charly Bailey
Designers Lisa Wyman and Alistair Barnes
Production Controller Ros Napper
Photographers Karl Adamson and Kim Sayer

Visit our website at www.davidandcharles.co.uk

David & Charles books are available from all good bookshops; alternatively you can contact
our Orderline on 0870 9908222 or write to us at FREEPOST EX2 110, D&C Direct, Newton Abbot,
TQ12 4ZZ (no stamp required UK only); US customers call 800-289-0963 and Canadian
customers call 800-840-5220.

Contents

Introduction

"Let yourself go with designs that are richer and more beautiful than ever before."

While it is important to remember the traditional rules of paperfolding, this book aims to give you the freedom to try new, sensational variations. If you love working with paper, you will surely be inspired by the many innovative projects, paperfolding styles and techniques presented here. Each project introduces and applies a new technique, or builds on a previous one, so that by the time you have worked through the book you will be amazed at how easy it is to create paperfolds of varying degrees of sophistication.

The projects in this book have been conceived for anyone who wants to make designs that are decorative and fun, geometric and stylized, multi-pieced or practical. Feel free to adapt any project to suit your requirements, or simply to experiment, which is the best way to discover new approaches and ideas. Above all, enjoy exploring the creative possibilities of working with paper.

Using this book

We suggest that you work through this book from beginning to end, starting with the first section, which introduces you to the most versatile of materials – paper and card. Here we list the essential tools and materials needed to get started and explain the basic folding symbols. These are the backbone of paperfolding and will enable you to make all the projects that follow. In this section we divulge a few secrets for folding paper correctly and explain the method for reverse folding.

Then, as you work through the projects section, chapter-by-chapter you will discover various styles of paperfolding, starting with tea bag folding and progressing to stylized tato-ori, iris folding, origami and the exciting possibilities of the techniques of tissue folding and modular origami. Each project lists all the materials you need, with photographs and step-by-step diagrams to help you achieve exquisite results. You'll also find a variety of ideas to help you adapt and personalize the projects and extend the range of possibilities. The projects are organized with the simplest or most fundamental techniques at the beginning. Some of the later sections have a basis in earlier projects, so we suggest that you work through them in order.

The final section of the book contains the templates and folding patterns you will need to complete some of the projects and includes a list of suppliers – which you may find useful when searching for appropriate tools and materials – and paperfolding societies.

We hope that our enthusiasm for all things paper will inspire your own creative adventure in making some – or all – of the projects. Are you ready to cross into a new dimension with just a few paper squares?

Steve and Megumi

Paper and Card

One of the greatest delights of paperfolding is the aesthetic and tactile enjoyment you will get from handling the amazingly rich diversity of paper types that are now widely available. Choosing colours and patterns to enhance each other and the quality of the proposed project can be as rewarding and stimulating as actually folding the object.

Origami paper can be purchased at stationery shops, Asian gift shops, toy stores, and craft supply stores. For papers and cards that have a textured or decorative surface, look in stationery stores and in those that carry craft supplies. For beautifully patterned paper, try using gift wrap from stationery stores. There you can also find pearlescent papers and paper-backed metallic foil. Or you can use a mail-order service or online shopping (see page 119 for a starting point in your hunt for resources).

All papers and cards have a grain. If you fold with the grain you can produce a nice, sharp crease, but if you fold against it you may struggle to achieve good results and you are likely to produce a more uneven edge. To find the grain, lightly bend card both widthways and lengthways and see in which direction it moves more easily.

Correct storage of paper and card is important and is often overlooked. Never leave large sheets rolled up for long periods, or they will not unroll later; never leave paper in strong sunlight, as it will fade; do not store it in a damp room, as the fibres will absorb moisture and warp the sheets. Instead, purchase a large, clear plastic document folder in which to store special papers, plus a box file for holding smaller sheets.

The fun starts with choosing what type of paper to fold. Matching the paper to the project is an exciting challenge, and in the finished pieces reproduced in this book you can see what we have used from our own collections to make the projects look their best. For practice, supplies of inexpensive papers are required. The best source is photocopier paper, obtainable from the quick print outlets that are found in most shopping centres or malls. Alternatively, computer paper and writing paper are good-quality practice papers.

Paper that flakes or splits at the crease when folded will be unsuitable for the projects in this book. Also, brightly coloured paper can make some designs look rather childish. With card you can usually feel if it will be strong enough to stand up to a little wear and tear, or if it's going to buckle once it has been decorated. Always buy the best materials you can afford. Quality shows and, in the long run, it saves time, money and effort. The following information may be helpful in choosing the best paper for each project.

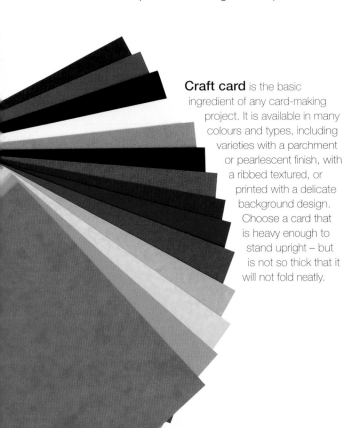

Craft card is the basic ingredient of any card-making project. It is available in many colours and types, including varieties with a parchment or pearlescent finish, with a ribbed textured, or printed with a delicate background design. Choose a card that is heavy enough to stand upright – but is not so thick that it will not fold neatly.

Duo paper has a different colour or shade on the reverse side. It is a great asset to the paper folder because it helps provide areas of alternate colour in the finished project.

Iris paper

comprises strips of thin coloured paper. Gift wrap is ideal, as long as it is not too thick because many layers are needed to make up the completed design. Patterned papers or those with abstract designs often work best.

Metallic foil, pearlescent and shiny papers

are some of the more difficult materials to work with, but if you persevere the end results can look quite spectacular. They are readily available in rolls along with other gift wraps, especially in gold, silver, green and red at Christmas.

Gift wrap

is a wonderful paper to work with, as it is often quite sturdy and nowadays there is so much choice around. Avoid glossed wrapping paper, which cracks along the fold-lines and tends to unfold.

Handmade paper

is often a softer and more fabric-like material than machine-made paper. Japanese washi and other handmade papers from around the world are left in a natural hue or given a solid colour, but much handmade paper is also made with exquisite designs and patterns, some of which are so elegant they almost appear to resemble brocade.

Textured paper

is available in a range of finishes, from smooth to rippled, wood-grained and even with animal-skin textures. It will make projects look extra special. **Vellum** is a translucent paper with a smooth finish. It comes in a variety of shades, patterns and embossed textures. Lighter-weight vellum is easiest to cut, score and fold, whereas heavier vellum works better for projects that need greater durability.

Tissue paper

is the most flimsy of all papers; the featherweight quality of tissue makes it almost translucent. The shades are strong, bordering on the iridescent, and dazzling combinations can be made. It is possible to buy packets of assorted colours of tissue paper.

Origami paper

is most readily available with a solid colour on one side and white on the reverse. Most packets contain a rainbow of colours although occasionally you may find packets containing only one colour. It takes a sharp fold without cracking or shedding flecks of colour.

Tea bag papers

can be used to make beautiful flower-like designs. Some sheets have just one design on them; others have two compatible designs. You can cut squares from gift wrap (as long as it has a repeat pattern) or, as in Hungary and the Netherlands, use the paper bags that encase herbal teas.

Basic Tool Kit

It is a good plan to begin by assembling a basic tool kit because this is the equipment you will use again and again. We have built up our tool kit over several years and are constantly adding to it. The items listed here are found in our tool kit and were used to create the projects in this book. You will need additional items for each project as well as the appropriate paper or card, and these are listed with the project instructions.

Eraser to remove guidelines. Choose one that will not leave marks on the paper or craft card.

Glue stick is a clean, quick and safe glue in a lipstick-type container. It is ideal for most light paper work. Take care that the glue does not smudge the design on printed papers. Be sure to replace the lid immediately after use, otherwise the glue stick will dry up.

PVA adhesive is a safe, ready-mixed white solution adhesive that becomes invisible when dry. A small amount can be poured into a saucer or dish and applied with a cocktail stick for delicate work. If applied in large amounts to paper it will make it waterlogged and crinkled. When gluing thin materials together ensure that the glue does not seep to the surface.

Hole punch for making holes in gift tags that can be threaded or to create decorative holes in paper.

Scissors You will need a large pair for trimming and a small pair for intricate work. Cutting adhesive tape or glued paper can leave a residue on the blades that may then transfer onto your work, so keep the blades clean.

Tweezers can be useful for pressing small folds into place and for picking up and positioning small punched paper shapes.

Masking tape for holding paper and templates in position. It is low-tack so it can be removed without marking the surface.

Sticky tape is ideal for sticking paper and mending light objects.

Double-sided tape is sticky on both sides and is ideal for mounting card onto card and for sticking background papers and tea bag rosettes to craft card. Cut it to length and stick it on like ordinary sticky tape, then remove the backing strip to reveal a second adhesive surface.

Self-healing cutting mat is the best surface for cutting on with a craft knife because the edges of the cut seal back up, or heal, so as not to leave an indent. The mat protects your working surface and has a resilience that makes cutting easier. However, the mat will only cope with vertical cuts – angled cuts will gouge out slithers or chunks.

Ruler for measuring and marking your material. If you also use it for cutting or scoring against, make sure you use a steel ruler or one with a metal edge. Always use a craft knife with a metal ruler – the knife can cut nicks in a plastic one, making it unusable.

Bone folder is a shaped tool that enables you to score and fold paper and card to give a crisp, professional finish.

Craft knife is often easier to use than a pair of scissors when cutting long straight lines or intricate curves. The best and cheapest are those in which the blade is located within the body of the knife and sections are snapped off as they wear down. You can also use a scalpel. Store with care by retracting the blade if possible or sticking it into a cork. Replace blades regularly as a blunt blade will not cut cleanly.

Pencils A 2B pencil is best for drawing and marking on your material because you can easily erase what you have drawn if you make a mistake. Use a white pencil to trace onto dark craft card.

Black felt-tip pen with a medium-sized tip is ideal for blocking in colour and for adding fine detail or drawing small motifs on a greetings card or gift tag.

Red ballpoint pen is invaluable for transferring a traced template onto your craft material.

Tracing paper is used to transfer templates onto your material. Airmail paper or greaseproof (waxed) paper can also be used.

Embellishments

Enhancing your projects with embellishments is the best part of papercrafting. Scan the aisles of your local craft shop and experiment with the vast array of colourful items that they have to offer. Store your decorative accessories in self-seal plastic bags to keep them clean and organized. Here are some of the items that we have found useful for adding that finishing touch.

Beads can be threaded onto different threads or wire, sewn or stuck to cards. They come in hundreds of colours and sizes. Seek them out in charity shops, cut them off old clothes or purchase them from haberdashery stores.

Decorative paper punches produce a hole and punched shape, either of which can be used in your projects. Hold the punch upside down so you can see where you are placing it.

Crystal glitter glue is fine glitter in glue. Use it directly from the squeezable bottle.

Mizuhiki are dyed cords of twisted paper used in Japanese gift wrapping. They usually come in pairs of colours: red and white, and gold and silver are the most auspicious combinations.

Craft stickers, crystals, foilart flowers, gems, jewels and shiny stars can usually be glued in place for added colour or sparkle.

Ribbons offer a frivolous change of texture to that special paperfolded project.

Adhesive foam pads are small pads with adhesive on both sides. They raise whatever is fixed to them away from the surface for a three-dimensional effect.

Craft stickers (peel-offs) come in as many different colours and designs as you can think of.

Deckle-edged scissors, also known as paper edgers, can add interest to a finished project. A light pencil line makes cutting accuracy easier.

Findings a general term for necklace clasps, brooch backs, earring wires and studs used to finish origami jewellery. There is a wide choice available.

Folding Symbols

The symbols that form the basis of the instructions in this book are used internationally. They show the direction in which the paper should be folded. If you are new to paperfolding, we suggest that you take a few squares of paper and study the following symbols and folding procedures before trying any of the projects. Look at the diagrams carefully to see which way the dashes, dots and arrows go over, through and under the paper/card, and fold your material accordingly.

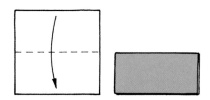

1 Valley fold Fold towards you or in front. This is shown in the diagrams by a line of dashes and a solid arrow showing the direction in which the paper has to be folded.

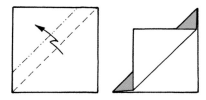

4 Step fold A zigzagged arrow drawn on top of the diagram means fold the paper in the direction shown by the arrow. A step fold is made by pleating the paper in a valley and mountain fold.

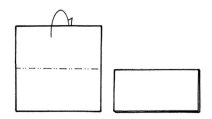

2 Mountain fold Fold away from you or behind. This is shown in the diagrams by a line of dots and dashes and a hollow-headed arrow. As in the valley fold, the arrow shows the direction in which the paper has to be folded.

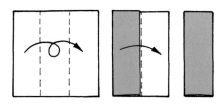

5 Fold over and over A looped arrow drawn on top of the diagram means keep folding the paper over in the direction shown by the arrow. Each fold-line represents one fold-over move.

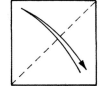

3 Fold and unfold An arrow that comes back on itself means fold, press flat and unfold the paper back to its previous position, as shown.

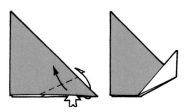

6 Outside reverse fold Solid and hollow-headed arrows and valley fold-lines instruct you to separate the layers of paper, taking one to the front and one to the back.

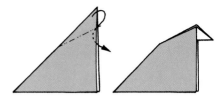

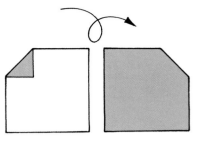

7 **Inside reverse fold** A wavy arrow with a broken tail and a mountain fold-line means push the point inside the model, in the direction indicated by the wavy arrow.

10 **Turn over** A looped arrow means turn the paper (or model) over in the direction shown by the arrow.

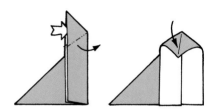

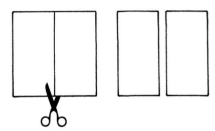

8 **Open and press** A hollow arrow with a short, indented tail instructs you to open the layers of paper and press them down neatly into the position shown in the diagram.

11 **Turn around** Two circling arrows means turn the paper (or model) around into the position shown.

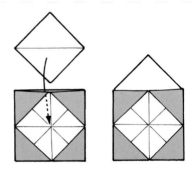

9 **Insert** An arrow with the tail broken near the head means insert the point into the pocket, as shown.

12 **Cut** A pair of scissors and a solid line means cut the paper. The solid line shows the position of the cut.

Helpful Tips

✿ If you find a special paper that you really like, buy several sheets and remember to make a note of the name of the shop or supplier. There is nothing more frustrating than finding that you only have a small corner of a particular paper left and not remembering where it came from.

✿ Avoid folding paper or cards that are coated on one side – they crack.

✿ Make sure that your working surface is level, smooth and uncluttered.

✿ Get yourself organized before you start a project. Have your basic tool kit ready (see page 8) plus any additional embellishments required.

✿ Clean up and clear everything away once you have finished the project in preparation for your next creative session.

✿ Read through the project instructions carefully before you begin. In the diagrams of this book, the shading represents the coloured side of the paper. Look at each diagram carefully to see what shape should be created when you have completed the step you are working on.

✿ To make the diagrams in each project clear, the paper is described as having a 'white' side and a 'coloured' side. Of course, depending on the type of paper you use for a particular project, the actual colours may be different.

✿ Above all, if a fold or whole project fails to work out, do not give up hope. Go through the diagrams one by one, checking that you have read the instructions correctly and have not missed an important word or overlooked a symbol. If you are still unable to complete the project, put it to one side and come back to it another day with a fresh mind.

How to Fold

In paperfolding it is important that all your folds are accurate. If not you will find it more difficult to complete the projects that follow and your results may be disappointing. So take several 15cm (6in) squares of origami paper and a little time to practice some basic folds before getting underway with the projects. Make all the creases in the paper by folding in a direction away from you, so making the folding easier and giving you more control over the paper. To produce sharp, flat folds, the flat surface of your fingernail is a great folding aid. If you prefer to use a folding tool, use a bone folder.

Creasing a Book Fold

The book fold is so named because once the paper is folded in half it resembles a book.

 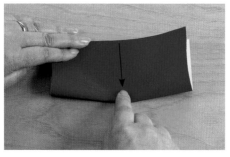 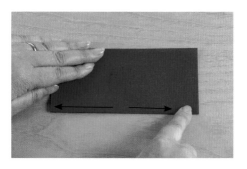

1 **To fold**, place one square of origami paper on your working surface, with the white side on top. Hold down the paper's top edge. Valley fold the bottom edge up to meet the top edge.

2 Keeping the edges together, run your forefinger down the paper's middle to the bottom edge to fix the middle of the fold.

3 To finish, run your forefinger along the bottom edge to both sides, pressing the fold into place and checking that the top edges are still aligned.

Creasing a Diaper Fold

When a square of paper is folded in half along its diagonal, or you have to make a fold in such a way, it is described as a 'diaper' fold – an American term that is now used internationally.

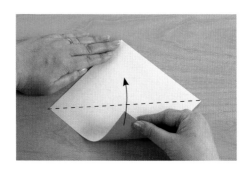 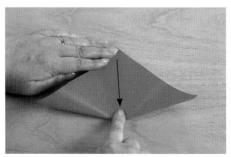 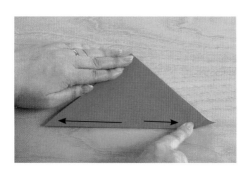

1 **To fold**, turn one square of origami paper around to look like a diamond, with the white side on top. Valley fold the bottom corner up to meet the top corner.

2 Keeping the corners together, run your forefinger down the paper's middle to the bottom edge to fix the middle of the fold.

3 To finish, run your forefinger along the bottom edge to both corners, pressing the fold into place and checking that the top corners are still aligned.

Open and Press

The open and press technique is not at all tricky to do. As open and press folds can come in many shapes and disguises, it is important to learn this technique carefully. Try the following on a square of origami paper diaper-folded in half.

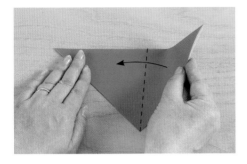

1 **To fold**, turn the diaper fold around so it points towards you. Valley fold in half from right to left.

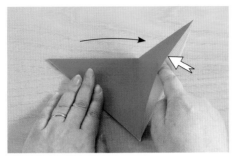

2 Lift the top half up along the middle fold-line.

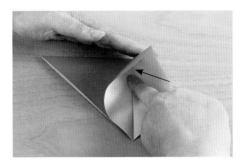

3 Insert your forefinger between the layers of paper. Start to open out the paper and ...

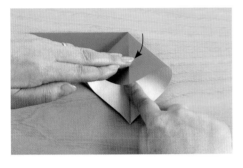

4 ... with your free hand press it down neatly ...

5 ... in a diamond shape. To finish, press the paper flat.

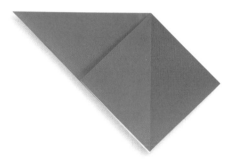

6 The finished fold should look like this.

Inside Reverse Fold

An inside reverse fold involves reversing a flap or point so that it is totally buried inside the model or protrudes out at the side. Try the following on a square of origami paper diaper-folded in half.

1 **To fold**, prepare your paper first by making a simple valley fold that will act as a pre-crease. Press the paper flat and unfold it.

2 Mountain fold and unfold on the same crease.

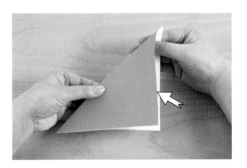

3 Separate the layers of paper and, using the fold-lines made in steps 1 and 2 as a guide, push ...

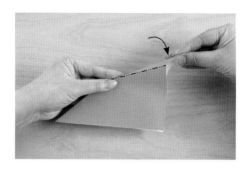

4 ... the paper down inside the model Begin to flatten your paper into the position shown in the photograph.

5 To finish, allow the layers to come back together as you flatten the paper. Notice that part of the paper that you reversed is now sandwiched between the outer layers of the paper.

6 The finished fold should look like this.

Outside Reverse Fold

This technique is similar to the inside reverse fold, except that the layers of paper are wrapped around the outside in order to effect the angle change. Try the following on a square of origami paper diaper-folded in half.

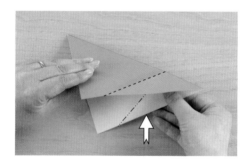

1 **To fold**, prepare your paper first by making a simple valley fold that will act as a pre-crease. Press the paper flat and unfold it.

2 Mountain fold and unfold on the same crease.

3 Separate the layers of paper and, using the fold-lines made in steps 1 and 2 as a guide, wrap ...

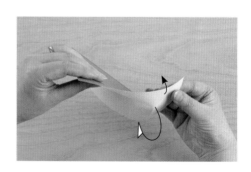

4 ... the end around the outside of the model, rather like turning up a cuff on a sleeve. Begin to flatten your paper into the position shown in the photograph.

5 To finish, allow the layers to come back together as you flatten the paper.

6 The finished fold should look like this.

Wrapping a Round Box

Cylindrical shapes appear often in commercial packaging and present their own wrapping problems. Here is the perfect wrap to give any round gift box an exciting new look. It is quite easy to do providing the required amount of paper is measured accurately.

you will need

A sheet of gift wrap in the following proportions:

Width: diameter of box plus its height

Length: diameter of box x 3.5

Two craft stickers

Length of gift ribbon the circumference of the box, plus a little extra

Basic tool kit

1 Place the gift wrap sideways on, with the plain side on top. Position the round box in the centre of the paper's width, as shown.

2 Valley fold in 1cm (³/₈in) of the right-hand side. Working from the left to right, roll the paper up tightly around the box, being careful to keep the lengths of paper at top and bottom even. Secure the overlap in place with a small piece of sticky tape.

3 On the bottom of the box, gradually fold in the paper over the rounded edge and towards the centre, creating small pleats to accommodate the extra paper.

4 Work all the way around in the same direction, spacing the pleats as evenly as possible. Press the pleats down firmly. Secure the centre with a craft sticker.

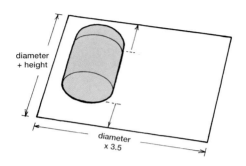

5 Stand the box upright and repeat step 3 on the top of the box.

6 Secure the centre with the remaining craft sticker. To finish, place the length of ribbon around the wrapped box and tie its ends together in a bow.

The wrapped box can then be completed with a stylish tea bag folded floret – see page 26 for project instructions.

Tea Bag Folding

Tea bag folding is a variation of origami and uses many of the same techniques as modular origami. The chosen fold is made several times using the required number of pieces of patterned squares and then each piece slides into the other to produce a rosette with a kaleidoscopic effect. It is believed that the craft originated in The Netherlands, when a Dutch crafter, Tiny Van Der Plas, was in need of a unique and decorative birthday card. As Tiny sat thinking, she began absently folding a colourful tea bag envelope and came up with various units that could be quickly transformed into decorative rosettes.

TOOLS

Paper
Some paper folders still use the traditional paper envelopes for tea bag folding, but these are not easily attainable. Now, however, decorated papers are commercially available for the craft. Some sheets have just one design on them; others have two different but compatible designs. You can also cut tea bag squares from origami paper, gift wrap, patterned papers or metallic foil. Just make sure that the paper is thin and can be folded easily.

Deckle-edged scissors
These scissors have blades with a decorative edge so that when paper is cut, a fancy 'deckled' edge is created. They will add interest to your completed designs and can also help to hide any folding mistakes.

TECHNIQUES

Assembling a rosette
When learning how to tea bag fold, it is usually best to start with 15cm (6in) squares, and then decrease the size of the squares when you are comfortable with the technique. The parts that make up a rosette must be assembled at the correct angles, making a tight circle. Any deviation will make it almost impossible to perform the final manoeuvre, and a lopsided or buckled rosette will result. For comfort and safety, work on a flat, clean surface taking care to keep sharp tools and glues well out of the reach of children.

Striped Rosette

Tea bag folding may look really difficult, but the folding technique is surprisingly easy and produces some pleasing results. The following project is based around a very easy unit fold. Try making it in several different colours to vary the finished rosette. For a successful end result, make your folds neat and precise.

you will need

Eight 7.5cm (3in) squares of flower-patterned origami paper

Basic tool kit

Striped rosette card
For a card, mount a square of blue craft card to a slightly larger square of light blue craft card. Place centrally on a yellow two-panel card and trim to fit. Glue the rosette on top and add gold peel-offs to finish.
Finished size of card:
21 x 14.8cm (8¼ x 5⅞in)

1 **To make the rosette**, valley fold one square of origami paper in half from bottom to top, with the patterned side on top. Valley fold in half from left to right.

2 Valley fold the front flap of paper in half from top right to bottom left.

3 Mountain fold the flap's bottom left hand corner behind in to the middle.

4 One unit completed. Repeat steps 1–3 with the remaining seven squares of origami paper.

5 Place one unit over another, as shown. Glue them together using a glue stick.

6 Keep on placing units over each other and gluing them together. To finish, slide the last unit underneath the first one and glue them together to form a circular floret-like design.

Rosette Greetings

If you are looking for a distinctive card for a truly special occasion, look no further than this glamorous tea bag design. A handmade card is a very tangible expression of your feelings for the person receiving it. It is clear that far more thought and time goes into a card that you have created yourself rather than one that is shop-bought, and the extra effort is sure to be appreciated. This stunning rosette design, mounted on sparkling craft net, will be treasured forever.

Blue rosette card

you will need

Dark blue two-panel card (see box below)

Eight 5cm (2in) squares of winter leaf tea bag paper

11cm (4⁵/₁₆in) square of light blue pearlescent craft card

13.5cm (5⁵/₁₆in) square of navy blue craft card

12.5cm (5in) square of silver craft fabric net

Blue sticky-backed gem

Crystal glitter glue

Craft stickers such as stars and snowflakes

Basic tool kit

TECHNIQUES

Making a two-panel card
All the cards in this book are created from an A4 (29.7 x 21cm / 11¾ x 8¼in) rectangle of craft card. The rectangle of card is turned sideways on, lightly scored down its vertical middle line, turned over and valley folded in half from left to right along the scored line.

The effect created by the tea bag folded winter leaf paper is cool and classic. The blue gem at the centre and pearlescent star mount add a real touch of sparkle.
Finished size of card: 21 x 14.8cm (8¼ x 5⅞in)

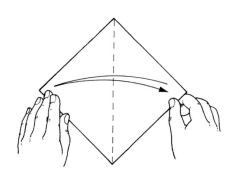 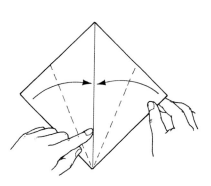 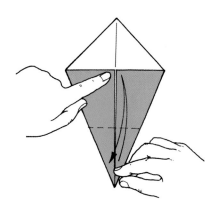

1 **To make the rosette**, turn one square of tea bag paper around to look like a diamond, with the white side on top. Fold and unfold in half from right to left.

2 From the bottom corner, valley fold the sloping edges in to meet the middle fold-line. Press them flat, making a kite base.

3 Valley fold the bottom point up to meet the horizontal edges. Press flat and unfold it.

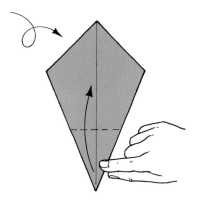 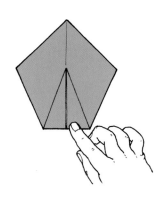 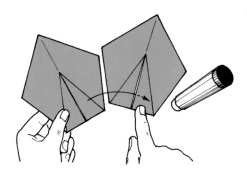

4 Turn the kite base over. Valley fold the bottom point up along the existing horizontal fold-line.

5 One unit completed. Repeat steps 1–4 with the remaining seven squares of tea bag paper.

6 Slot one unit inside another, as shown. Glue them together.

  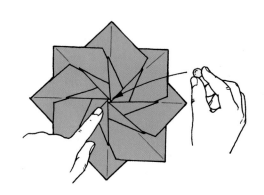

7 Slot and glue another unit into place.

8 Keep on slotting and gluing units together to form a circular rosette-like design.

9 Place the blue sticky-backed gem in to the rosette's centre.

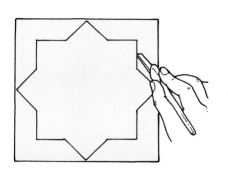 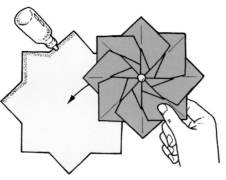 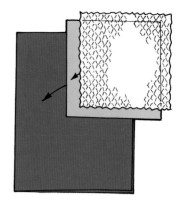

10 **To make a card**, trace the rosette's template from page 117 and transfer it onto the light blue pearlescent craft card. Using the craft knife, cutting mat and metal ruler, cut out the eight-pointed star.

11 Apply glue to the back of the rosette and mount it centrally on the front of the star. Apply a line of crystal glitter glue around the edges of the star.

12 Apply glue to the back of the silver fabric net and mount it centrally on the navy blue craft card and stick this to the front of the dark blue two-panel card, slightly below the card's top edge, as shown.

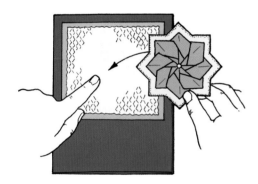 

13 Apply glue to the back of the star and mount it centrally on the fabric net.

14 To finish, complete the decorations with star and snowflakes stickers, as shown.

Gold rosette card
This variation of the main design is made using wine striped tea bag paper with a gold craft pearl glued to the centre, and mounted on a square of gold spider web paper. A length of ribbon was glued to a strip of gold paper and placed centrally down a warm-yellow two-panel card, with the rosette then mounted onto this. It is embellished with decorative gold leaves and triangular mounts for an opulent look.
Finished size of card: 21 x 14.8cm (8¼ x 5⅞ in)

Star Decorations

The star is based around a very easy unit. Make them in a variety of colours and sizes for the best effect. When folded out of duo paper the star makes an ideal decoration or gift tag. Stunning stars will add style to your Christmas trimmings and are one of the most easily recognizable symbols of the season. However, they could also be adapted to use for a themed birthday party.

Christmas stars

you will need

Sticky-backed gems

Gold thread

Basic tool kit

For the large star

Eight 6cm (2³/₈in) squares of red and green duo paper

For the small star

Eight 5cm (2in) squares of red and gold duo paper

When made in traditional festive colours, the stars can be threaded with gold thread to hang on the Christmas tree, or used to add a creative touch to your gift wrapping. However you choose to use them, they are sure to be a talking point. All stars are folded in exactly the same way.

Finished size of large star: 13 x 13cm (5 x 5in)

Finished size of small star: 9 x 9cm (3½ x 3½in)

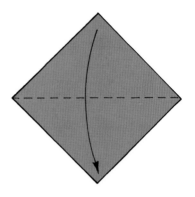

1 **To make the star,** turn one square of duo paper around to look like a diamond, with the red side on top. Valley fold in half from top to bottom.

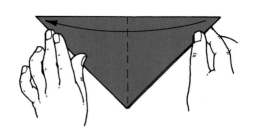

2 Valley fold in half from right to left.

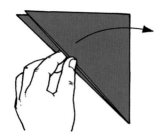

3 Lift the top half up along the middle fold-line.

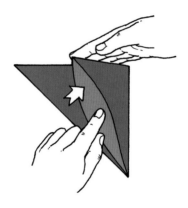

4 Open out the paper and …

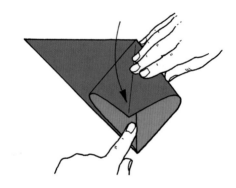

5 … press it down neatly in a diamond shape.

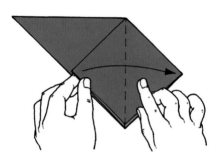

6 Valley fold the diamond in half from left to right.

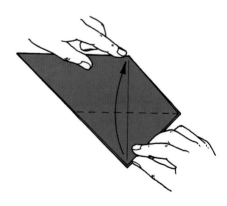

7 Valley fold the front flap of paper in half from bottom to top.

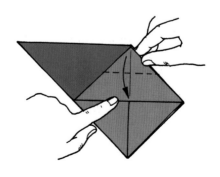

8 Valley fold the flap's tip in to the middle.

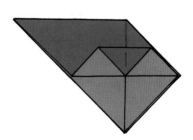

9 One unit completed. Repeat steps 1–8 with the remaining seven squares of duo paper.

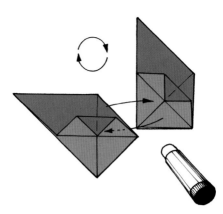 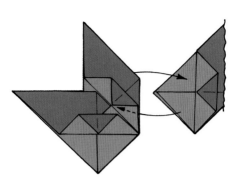 

10 Turn two units around into the position shown. Slot one unit inside the other. Glue them together.

11 Keep on slotting and gluing units together to form a circular star-like design.

12 Place the sticky-backed gem in to the star's centre. To finish, attach a loop of gold thread to the star, so that you can hang it from a Christmas tree, if desired.

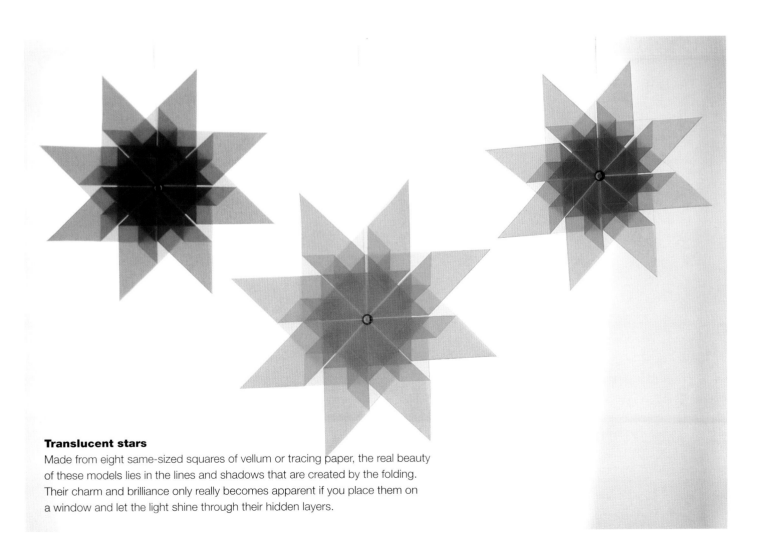

Translucent stars

Made from eight same-sized squares of vellum or tracing paper, the real beauty of these models lies in the lines and shadows that are created by the folding. Their charm and brilliance only really becomes apparent if you place them on a window and let the light shine through their hidden layers.

Floret Wrapping

Cylindrical containers are notoriously difficult to wrap, yet many gifts are packaged in this way, including sweets and biscuits, bottles of drink or perfume, golf balls, posters and chocolates. Using the simple yet ingenious technique shown on page 15 you will be able to wrap any tube perfectly, then use a stylish tea bag folded floret to conceal the joins at the top, and finish off the wrapping with a flourish. Florets can be used to decorate any wrapped gift, and are an ideal personalized alternative to a ribbon rosette.

Floret box decoration

you will need

12cm (4¾in) in diameter circular gift box optionally wrapped in brown and gold handmade paper (see page 15)

Eight 7.5cm (3in) squares of rainbow-patterned tea bag paper

5cm (2in) in diameter circle of pink craft card for the floret base

Three-dimensional craft flower

Deckle-edged scissors

Basic tool kit

Floret card

A smaller version of the floret decoration can be used to make a special card. A few strategically placed lengths of ribbon and some three-dimensional craft flowers, and you have created a personalized gift card. Try your own preferred papers to make the card even more individual. See page 29 for project instructions.

Finished size of card: 21 x 14.8cm (8¼ x 5⅞in)

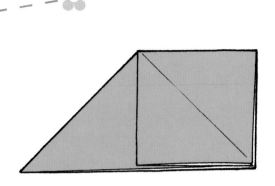

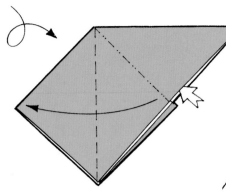

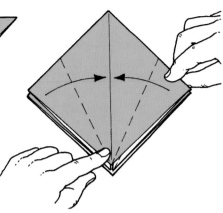

1 **To make the floret box decoration,** repeat steps 1–5 for the Christmas star on page 24 with one square of tea bag paper, but with the white side on top in step 1.

2 Turn the paper over. Lift the top half up along the middle fold-line. Open out the paper and press it down neatly in a diamond shape, making a preliminary fold.

3 From the bottom point, valley fold the lower (open) sloping edges in to meet the middle fold-line.

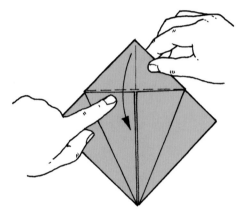

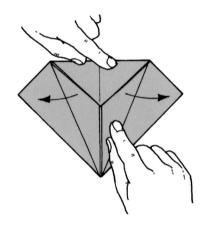

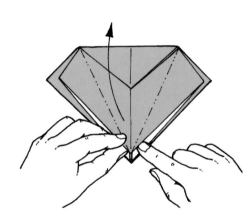

4 The paper should now look like an ice cream cone, with a triangle of ice cream at the top and the cone below. Valley fold the 'ice cream' down and over the cone.

5 Unfold the edges from underneath the 'ice cream' as if opening the doors of a cupboard. Now make a petal fold. This is what you do: …

6 … pinch and lift up the front flap of paper.

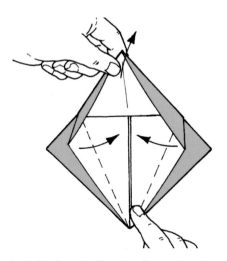

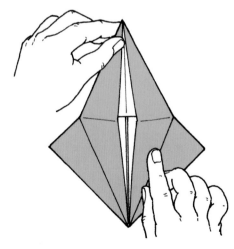

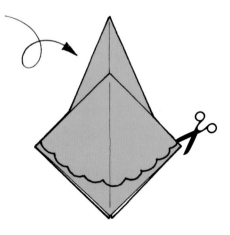

7 Continue to lift up the flap, so its edges meet in the middle.

8 Press the paper flat, making it diamond shaped. This completes the petal fold.

9 Turn the paper over. Using the deckle-edged scissors, cut along the paper's lower sloping edges, as shown, to complete one decorative unit. Repeat steps 1–9 with the remaining seven squares of paper.

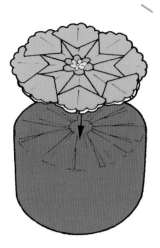

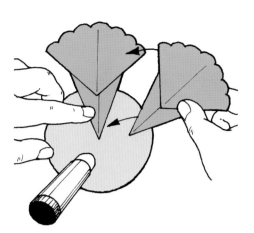

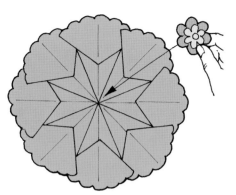

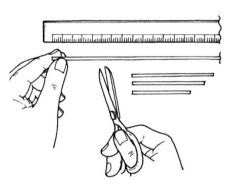

10 Turn all the units around into the position shown. Apply glue to the back of one unit at the pointed end and attach it to the pink circle's centre. Repeat with another unit, positioning it adjacent to the previous one, while allowing its deckled edge to overlap, as shown.

11 Keep on gluing and positioning units side by side to form a circular floret-like design. Remove the backing from the three-dimensional craft flower and attach it at the floret's centre.

12 To finish, apply double-sided tape to the back of the floret base and mount it centrally on top of the circular gift box. For instructions on how to wrap a circular gift box, see page 15.

Floret card

you will need

Burgundy two-panel card

Eight 5cm (2in) squares of flower-patterned tea bag paper

3cm (1¼in) in diameter circle of pink craft card for the floret base

50cm (19¾in) length of 0.3cm (⅛in) wide cream ribbon

Seven three-dimensional craft flowers

Deckle-edged scissors

Crystal glitter glue

Basic tool kit

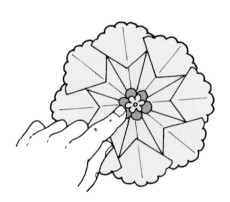

1 **To make the floret card,** begin by repeating steps 1–11 for the floret box decoration with the eight squares of tea bag paper, deckle-edged scissors, circle of craft card and one three-dimensional flower.

2 Cut the ribbon into six different sized lengths, for example 5cm (2in), 6cm (2⅜in), 7cm (2¾in), 9cm (3½in), 10cm (4in) and 12cm (4¾in).

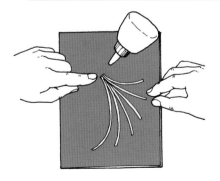

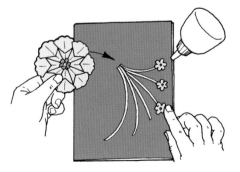

3 Starting with the shortest length first and progressing in order of size, carefully glue the lengths of ribbon to the front of the burgundy two-panel card, fanning them out, as shown.

4 Apply glue to the back of the floret base and mount it on top of the fanned out ribbons, covering up their 'joined' ends. Remove the backing from the remaining six three-dimensional craft flowers and attach a flower over the 'free' end of each ribbon, as shown.

5 To finish, complete the decorations with dabs of crystal glitter glue to suggest drops of dew.

Tato-ori

A tato is a type of Japanese folded wrapper used for holding small household items such as needles, ends of thread, buttons and stamps. Tato often take on the form of hexagonal or octagonal stylized flower patterns. Many of these models have a wonderful spring action – when you tug on their flaps they stretch open and then spring back to a closed position, very much like the traditional Moroccan leather purse. The Japanese origami master, Michio Uchiyama, developed styles of four, six and eight-sided tato, made entirely without cutting. Michio's son, Kosho, continued developing patterns for tato that focused on twisting and more three-dimensional folds. Many different modern-day tato have been designed to hold CDs, business cards, sheets of paper, gifts and cherished photographs.

TOOLS

Paper
There are no hard and fast rules regarding choice of paper, but do consider that the colours of traditional origami paper can be too harsh for some tato. Washi and other handmade papers give a light crease to your folding and a softer, less angular look to your finished tato. Gift wrap is a wonderful paper to fold with, as it is often quite sturdy and there is so much choice around. Try using textured paper for that special tato; there are many different kinds of paper available that have exquisite designs printed on them. Duo paper, however, helps provide areas of alternate colour to finished tato.

Mizuhiki
Tato-ori does not require any investment in specialized tools. You will already have the tools needed in your basic tool kit; but one item of equipment that will probably involve a trip to a craft supply store is mizuhiki. These dyed cords of twisted paper come in long lengths, which can easily be cut to size. Craft stores also supply cheaper varieties of mizuhiki consisting of thin paper foil wrapped around a twisted paper core. In the projects that follow, you can successfully substitute ribbon or gift wrapping cord for mizuhiki if you are struggling to find them.

Envelope Tato

This envelope, probably the most basic of tato designs, is made by folding a square of paper around a greetings card, and is ideal to learn the basic technique before beginning the projects in this section. With just a few changes to the dimensions of the paper it is possible to fold an envelope to fit any sized card. The tato can be folded from fine textured Japanese handmade papers or decorative Western papers. Use high-quality paper to protect your creations if you are sending them by post.

you will need

35.5cm (14in) square of handmade paper

Craft sticker

Two-panel card of your choice (to enclose within the envelope)

Basic tool kit

1 Turn the square of handmade paper around to look like a diamond, with the plain side on top. Turn the two-panel card sideways on and place it on the paper, towards the bottom corner. Valley fold the bottom corner up and over the card.

2 Valley fold the left-hand corner in and over the card.

3 Valley fold the right-hand corner in and over the card.

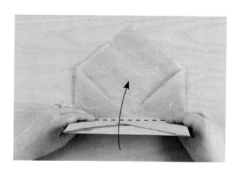

4 Valley fold the wrapped card up along its horizontal top edge, as shown.

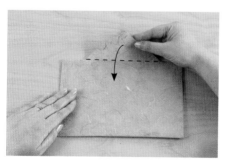

5 Valley fold the top point down and over the card.

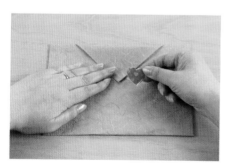

6 To finish, fasten the point down with a craft sticker.

T-shirt Disc Cases

This bright and cheerful shirt is easy to make and once completed you can slide a CD or DVD easily under its folds with no glue or tape needed. It is our interpretation of a model originally taught to us by Toshie Takahama. For a football or rugby fan, fold it from paper in the particular colour of the strip worn by their favourite team. You can vary the look of the shirt by adding a white border to the collar and sleeves. A matching gift tag is made from a 16 x 24cm (6¼ x 9½in) rectangle of red paper. A ribbon tie completes the look.

Sports shirt CD cases

you will need

Basic tool kit

For the plain sports shirt

26 x 36.5cm (10¼ x 14³⁄₈in) sheet of gift wrap

12cm (4¾in) square of craft card to back the CD

For sports shirt with white collar and cuffs

26 x 38.5cm (10¼ x 15¹⁄₈in) sheet of gift wrap with a white (plain) back

12cm (4¾in) square of craft card to back the CD

Funky shirts

These CD cases do not have to be on a sports theme. Simply by choosing a different patterned paper you can make a case for any recipient. The shirt can be also filled with letters, photographs and other mementos but make sure the items are not too bulky or it may tear.

Finished size of CD case: 14.5 x 19cm (5¾ x 7½in)
Finished size of gift tag: 9.5 x 12.5cm (3¾ x 5in)

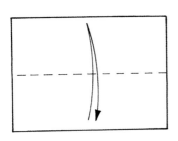

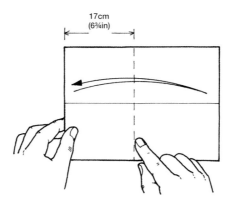

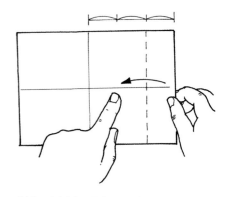

1 **To make the plain sports shirt**, place the gift wrap sideways on, with the white side on top. Fold and unfold in half from bottom to top.

2 Valley fold in 17cm (6¾in) of the left hand side. Press flat and unfold it.

3 Valley fold the right-hand side over to a point one-third of the way to the fold-line made in step 2.

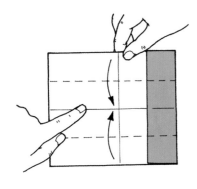

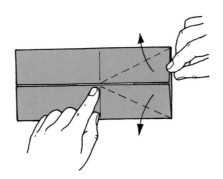

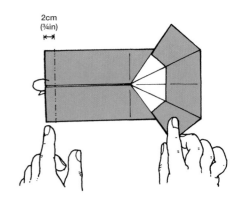

4 Valley fold the top and bottom edges in to the middle.

5 Valley fold the middle right-hand corners out on a slant, as shown, making the shirt's sleeves.

6 Mountain fold behind 2cm (¾in) of the left-hand side.

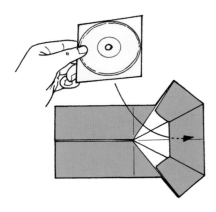

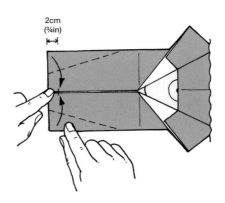

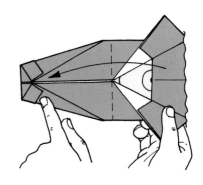

7 At this stage in the folding, tuck your CD or DVD along with the square of craft card underneath the right-hand band of paper.

8 Valley fold the top and bottom left-hand corners in on a slant to meet the middle edges at a point that is 2cm (¾in) away from the side, making the shirt's collar.

9 With a valley fold, tuck the sleeves …

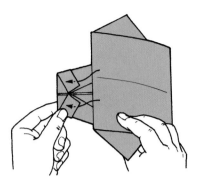

10 ... underneath the collar.

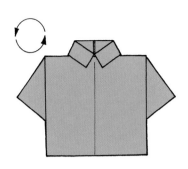

11 To finish, turn the paper around into the position shown.

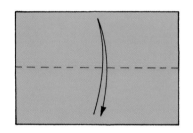

1 **To make the sports shirt with white collar and cuffs**, place the gift wrap sideways on, with the coloured side on top. Fold and unfold in half from bottom to top.

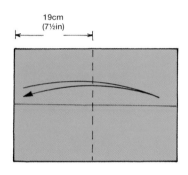

19cm (7½in)

2 Valley fold in 19cm (7½in) of the left hand side. Press flat and unfold it.

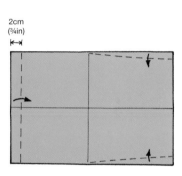

2cm (¾in)

3 Valley fold in 2cm (¾in) of the left-hand side. Valley fold a little of the top and bottom right-hand edges over on a slant, as shown, making ...

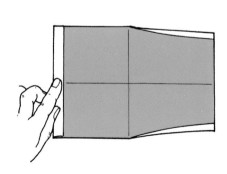

4 ... the start of the shirt's white collar and cuffs.

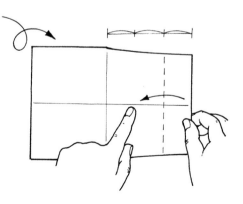

5 Turn the paper over. Repeat steps 3–11 of the plain sports shirt.

6 The completed shirt.

Special Sachets

This eye-catching tato was originally used to contain a sewing kit. Nowadays it can also hold romantic keepsakes, photographs of treasured moments or theatre tickets within its folds. As two squares of paper, glued back to back, are required to make this delightful tato, try combining a geometric print and a solid colour or experimenting with your favourite patterns and colours. When learning how to achieve this design, use 15cm (6in) squares of origami paper, progressing to larger-sized papers when you are comfortable with the folding technique.

Flat-pack sachets

you will need

Basic tool kit

For the small sachet

21cm (8¼in) square of wine handmade paper

21cm (8¼in) square of marble handmade paper

45cm (17¾in) length of 0.8cm (5/16in) wide wine ribbon

For the large sachet

25cm (10in) square of wood-patterned brown paper

25cm (10in) square of black leather gift wrap

Four 90cm (35½in) cords of mizuhiki – two each in gold and gold and green

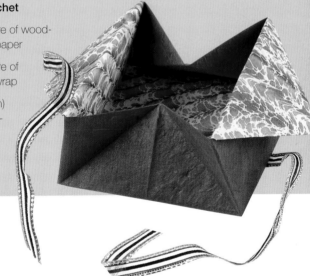

These ingenious sachets can be used to hold any item you desire. They are perfect for wrapping gifts, such as a bracelet or necklace, or tickets for a concert. Alternatively make them for yourself to keep your own treasures safe. Both the sachets are folded in the same way.
Finished size of small sachet: 7.5 x 7.5cm (3 x 3in)
Finished size of large sachet: 9 x 9cm (3½ x 3½in)

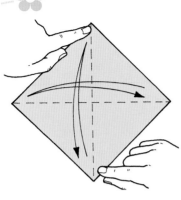

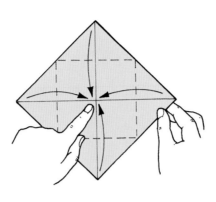

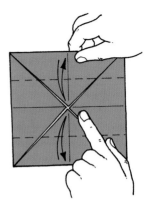

1 **To make a sachet**, glue the two same sized squares of paper back to back. From now onwards treat **both** layers of paper as if they were one. Turn the square around to look like a diamond, with the colour required for the inside of the box on top. Valley fold the opposite corners together in turn to mark the diagonal fold-lines, then open up again.

2 Valley fold the corners in to the middle, making a blintz base.

3 Valley fold the top and bottom edges in to the middle. Press flat and unfold them.

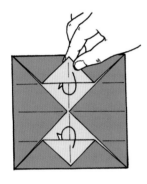

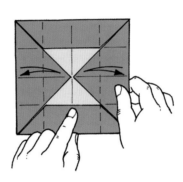

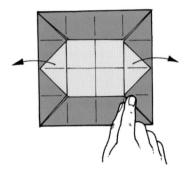

4 With a mountain fold, tuck the top and bottom triangles underneath their adjoining sections of paper, as shown.

5 Valley fold the sides in to the middle. Press flat and unfold them.

6 Unfold the right and left-hand sections of paper.

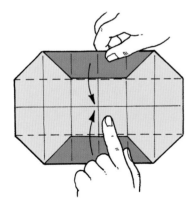

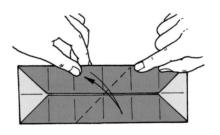

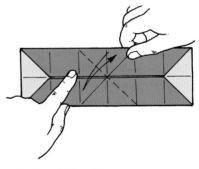

7 Valley fold the top and bottom edges in to the middle.

8 In the middle of the paper make a diagonal valley fold that runs from top right to bottom left, as shown. Press flat and unfold it.

9 In the middle of the paper make a diagonal valley fold that runs from top left to bottom right, as shown. Press flat and unfold it.

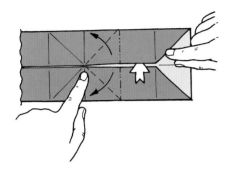

10 Using the valley folds made in steps 8 and 9 as a guide, reach inside and open out the right-hand layers of paper, simultaneously …

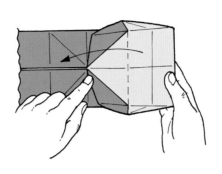

11 … valley folding the adjoining side over to lie along the middle edges.

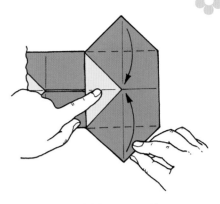

12 Valley fold the top and bottom corners in to meet the intersection of the adjacent fold-lines, as shown.

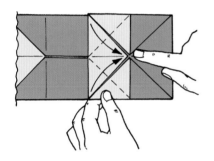

13 Valley fold the two middle corners in to meet the intersection of the adjacent fold-lines, as shown, making a point.

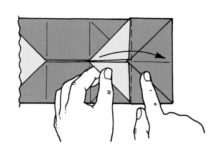

14 Valley fold the point over to meet the adjacent side.

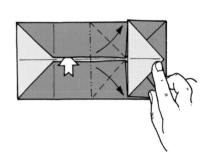

15 Repeat steps 10–14 with the left hand layers of paper.

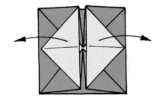

16 The completed flat packed sachet. Pull opposite points apart …

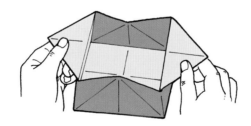

17 … and the sachet will open; release them and it will return to its original shape.

18 A ribbon or mizuhiki bow makes a lovely finishing touch and will help in keeping the sachet closed.

Treasures Tato

This delightful tato is the perfect wrap in which to store those cherished mementos that surround special memories. It is a place to keep souvenirs safe such as congratulations cards, confetti, birth records and photographs of family and friends. The tato's diamond-shaped flaps can carry a little extra something – perhaps a card or a small flower – and this surprise element makes it a joy to open. Try decorating your finished tato with pretty three-dimensional flower craft stickers.

Self-closing tato purse

you will need

20cm (8in) square of gold paper with a white back

Basic tool kit

This special purse can be used for personal use to protect your own treasured mementos, or would make a lovely wrap for confetti to give to guests to at a wedding.

Finished size of tato purse: 12 x 11.5cm (4¾ x 4½in)

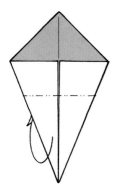

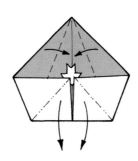

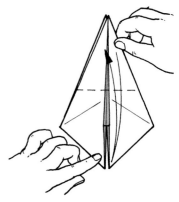

1 **To make the purse,** begin by repeating steps 1 and 2 for the rosette on page 20 with the gold square of paper, but with the coloured side on top in step 1. Mountain fold the kite base in half from bottom to top.

2 Pull the right and left-hand flaps of paper down towards you so their sloping edges come to rest along the middle fold-line. Press them flat, making a fish base.

3 Valley fold the front flap of paper in half from top to bottom. Press flat and unfold it.

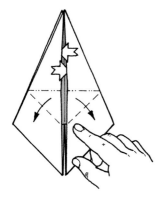

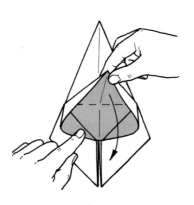

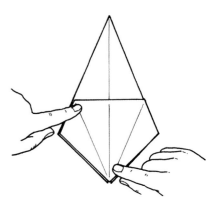

4 Using the valley fold made in step 3 as a guide, reach inside and open out the layers of the front flap, simultaneously …

5 … valley folding its tip down …

6 … to meet the bottom points. Press the paper flat.

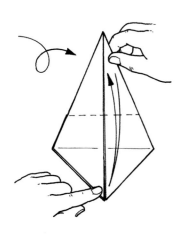

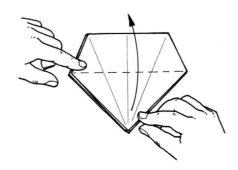

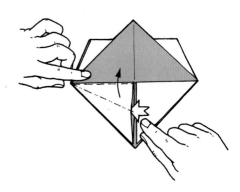

7 Turn the paper over. Repeat steps 3–6.

8 Valley fold the front flap of paper up on a line between the two side points, as shown.

9 Open out the left-hand point and press it down neatly in a diamond shape.

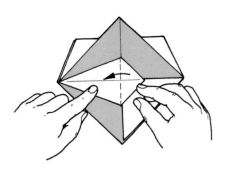

10 Valley fold the diamond's tip over as shown, making a triangle.

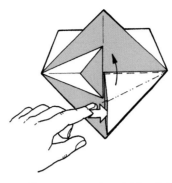

11 Repeat steps 9 and 10 with the right-hand point.

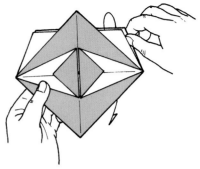

12 Fold the top edge of the back flap down on a line between the two side points, as shown.

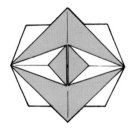

13 The completed tato.

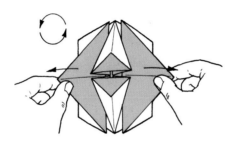

14 To open, turn the tato around into the position shown. Pull opposite triangular flaps apart …

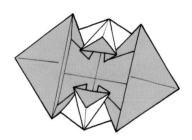

15 … and the tato will open; release them and it will return to its original shape.

Scrapbook tato

Tato can be used on scrapbook pages to hold special items. This baby-themed scrapbook page has a tato that could contain the birth announcement, the baby's first photographs or any other cherished items. You could even create tato using papers that co-ordinate with the nursery. This is the perfect way to save those precious moments, so that one day you can give them to your grown-up child.

Iris Folding

Iris folding is a papercrafting technique that originated in the Netherlands. Colour co-ordinated strips of folded paper are glued around a template, creating a spiralling design that resembles the iris of an eye or camera. An appropriate pattern is taped to the front of a pre-cut design opening and folded strips of coloured papers are layered and glued in position over the pattern from the back, making a spiral. The pattern is then gently removed and turned over to reveal the neat iris-folded paper design surrounded by the hand-cut frame. When you have mastered the basic overlapping technique, you can enjoy creating your own designs in hand-cut shaped apertures.

TOOLS

Paper and card

Originally, Dutch crafters would cut their strips from envelopes with patterned interiors, but now it is common to use lightweight papers, including those used for origami, to create iris-folded designs. The sheer number of patterns and colours available of papers suitable for iris folding can be overwhelming. Books or packs of papers specially designed for iris folding can be easily obtained from any craft outlet. Alternatively, you can use packaged origami paper or sheets of coloured gift wrap, and mix and match. Holographic papers or craft stickers add impact to the centre of your iris-folded design. The basic ingredient of any card-making project is the card stock itself. Card is available in many colours and types, some with a metallic finish, corrugated, or printed with a delicate design. When deciding what kind of card to use, remember that the finished design can be heavy so a thicker card is better.

Cutting equipment

The most important tools for iris folding are a self-healing cutting mat, craft knife and metal ruler. The cutting mat is an expensive item, but it will last for many years without becoming deeply scarred. It has grid lines printed upon it, which can help when you are ruling paper and card. A craft knife and metal ruler are ideal for cutting out apertures and paper strips. You will also need a small pair of good-quality, fine-pointed scissors for trimming the paper strips used in iris folding.

Transferring a design

Iris folding requires the use of templates. The projects in this chapter all use templates that can be found on pages 114–118. The templates shown are full size, but to make the projects you will need to transfer them to your paper or card.

1   **To transfer a design**, place a piece of tracing paper over the required template and, using small pieces of masking tape, hold it in place.

2   Using a 2B pencil, draw carefully around the illustrated template.

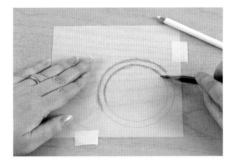

3   Remove the masking tape and tracing paper from the template and turn the tracing over. Using the pencil, go over the back of the traced outline. If you want to trace on to dark card, use a white pencil.

4   Turn the tracing paper back over. Re-using the pieces of masking tape, attach the tracing paper in the required position on your paper or card.

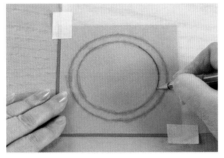

5   Using a red ballpoint pen, go around the traced outline again, pressing firmly to transfer the template.

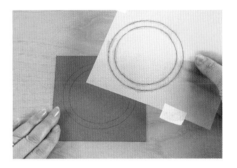

6   To finish, gently remove the masking tape and tracing paper.

Cutting and preparing strips

Iris folding requires the use of paper strips to create the designs. To make the projects you will need to either buy ready-made paper strips, or create your own, following this method.

1   **To prepare your strips**, place the iris papers sideways on, with their white side on top. Valley fold each one in half from top to bottom.

2   Cut the iris papers into 5cm (2in) strips.

3   Group them together by colour and in the order you wish to use them, so that once you get started on the design, everything is to hand and logically arranged.

Spiralling Baubles

These glittering baubles are the perfect decoration for parties or receptions. As they are made from paper they can be placed in a prominent position, high up where they will not be damaged by your guests, who will inevitably want to reach out and touch them. Iris-folded baubles can also be suspended by a ribbon or decorative thread from a Christmas tree, making a dazzling centrepiece. Alternatively the finished baubles can just as easily be turned into an eye-catching card.

Bauble

you will need

9cm (3½in) square of white craft card

10cm (4in) square of dark blue craft card

Five 2 x 40cm (¾ x 15¾in) rectangles of paper for the iris folds – one each in dark blue, light turquoise, dark blue with a white flower motif, light blue and pearlescent

2cm (¾in) square of silver paper

Lavender sticky-backed gem star

30cm (12in) length of 0.8cm (5/16in) wide blue ribbon

Crystal glitter glue

Basic tool kit

For the hanging bauble

3cm (1¼in) length of 24-gauge silver wire

Silver thread

For the card

Navy blue two-panel card

5 x 18cm (2 x 7in) rectangle of silver craft card

13 x 18.5cm (5⅛ x 7¼in) rectangle of dark blue craft card

13.5 x 19cm (5⁵/16 X 7½in) rectangle of white craft card

10cm (4in) length of 0.8cm (5/16in) wide blue ribbon

Christmas-themed stickers such as stars and baubles

Bauble card

Once you get the hang of this technique you will find it completely addictive. What better way to use your bauble creations than on a handmade card? See page 49 for project instructions.
Finished size of hanging bauble: 9 x 10cm (3½ x 4in)
Finished size of card: 21 x 14.8cm (8¼ x 5⅞in)

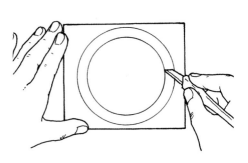

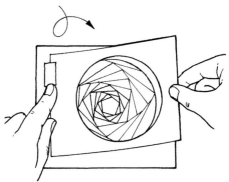

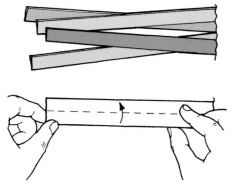

1 **To prepare**, trace the bauble template from page 115 and transfer it onto the square of white craft card. Using the craft knife and cutting mat, cut out the bauble's aperture.

2 Turn the aperture over and line it up with the folding pattern on page 115. Use small pieces of masking tape to hold the aperture in place on top of the pattern. You can use the pattern directly from the page or photocopy or trace it first.

3 Place the iris papers sideways on, with their white side on top. Valley fold each one in half from bottom to top.

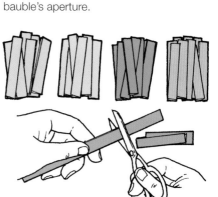

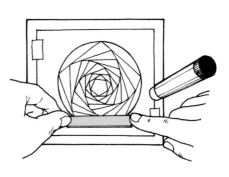

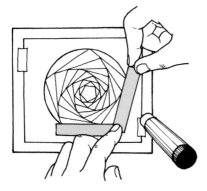

4 Cut the iris papers into 5cm (2in) strips. Group them together by colour and in the order you wish to use them.

5 **To begin iris folding**, first apply a line of glue around the aperture, adjacent to section 1* of the folding pattern. Try not to smear any glue onto the pattern. Take a strip of your first colour, position it exactly over section 1*, with its folded edge facing towards the middle and glue in place.

6 Take a strip of your second colour and, working anti-clockwise; place it over the pattern's outer section marked with a 2, and glue in place. Repeat with strips of your third, fourth and fifth colours, positioning and gluing them in place over sections 3, 4 and 5 respectively. You have made one 'round' of the pattern.

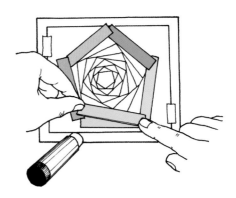

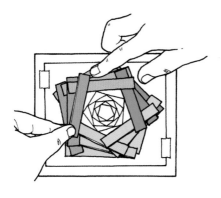

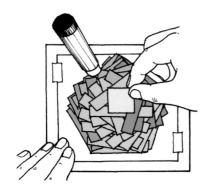

7 Start the next round with a strip of your first colour, applying glue to the previous strip when you stick the next one in place.

8 Continue working anti-clockwise around the folding pattern, taking a coloured strip from each of the groups in turn and making one full round each time until you reach the middle.

9 Glue the silver square over the centre hole.

10 Apply double-sided tape to the back of the iris folding, as shown, to hold all the strips in place.

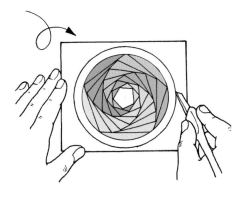

11 Remove the iris folding from the pattern and turn it over to reveal the folding in its aperture. Using the craft knife and cutting mat, cut around the bauble's outer edge, cutting through all layers as one.

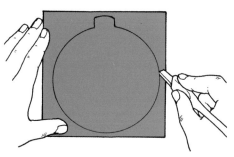

12 **To complete the bauble**, trace the bauble mat template from page 115 and transfer it onto the square of dark blue craft card. Using the craft knife and cutting mat, cut out the mat.

13 Remove the backing from the strips of double-sided tape on the back of the bauble and mount it centrally on the mat. Place the lavender sticky-backed gem star in to the bauble's centre.

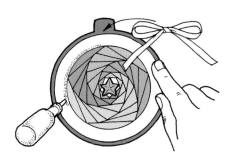

14 Make a bow with a 30cm (12in) length of blue ribbon and attach it to the front of the bubble, slightly below the bauble's top point, as shown. To finish, go around the inside edge of the bauble's aperture with crystal glitter glue.

15 **To make a hanging bauble**, using the pliers, bend the silver wire in to a loop. Firmly glue the loop using PVA adhesive to the back of the bauble, slightly below the bauble's top point. Attach a loop of silver thread to the bauble so that you can hang it from a Christmas tree, if desired.

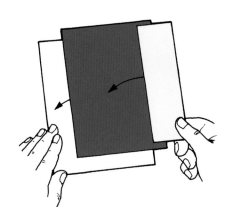

16 **To make a card**, turn the rectangles of silver, dark blue and white craft card lengthways on. Apply glue to the back of the silver card and mount it centrally on the dark blue card and stick this to the centre of the white card.

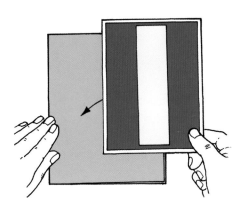

17 Apply glue to the back of the white card and mount it centrally on the front of the navy blue two-panel card.

18 Apply glue to the 10cm (4in) length of blue ribbon, turn it lengthways on and mount it centrally on the front of the two-panel card. Stick the back of the bauble to the card, slightly over the ribbon's lower end, as shown. To finish, complete the decorations with Christmas-themed stickers and crystal glitter glue.

Heartfelt Wishes

A Valentine's gift or card to the one you love is more thoughtful and personal when presented as an exquisite handmade token of affection. But you don't need to wait until Valentine's Day to transform your favourite papers into a lovely keepsake. This versatile iris-folded heart can be used for many different occasions, and can adorn not only cards, but also gift boxes and even scrapbook pages.

Valentine's card

you will need

Black two-panel card

6.5 x 8cm (2⅝ x 3⅛in) rectangle of black craft card

7 x 9cm (2¾ x 3½in) rectangle of red craft card

Four 2 x 40cm (¾ x 15¾in) rectangles of rose patterned paper for the iris folds – one each in rose, pink, cream and orange

2cm (¾in) square of silver paper

6.5 x 8.5cm (2⅝ x 3⅜in) rectangle of rose patterned paper

4 x 21cm (1½ x 8¼in) rectangle of gold spider web paper

21cm (8¼in) length of 0.3cm (⅛in) wide red ribbon

Silver sticky-backed gem heart

Red craft bow

Crystal glitter glue

Magical-themed stickers such as doves, top hats and stars

Basic tool kit

Wedding card

Using romantic colours and two hearts you can make the perfect card to send your congratulations to a newly engaged couple. For a marriage invitation, choose colours that match the bride's or the bridesmaids' dresses, to create a co-ordinating and unique keepsake for this once-in-a-lifetime occasion.
Finished size of both cards: 21 x 14.8cm (8¼ x 5⅞in)

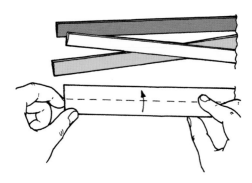

1 **To prepare**, trace the heart template from page 115 and transfer it onto the black craft card. Using the craft knife and cutting mat, cut out the heart's aperture.

2 Turn the aperture over and line it up with the folding pattern on page 115. Use small pieces of masking tape to hold the aperture in place on top of the pattern.

3 Place the iris papers sideways on, with their white side on top. Valley fold each one in half from bottom to top.

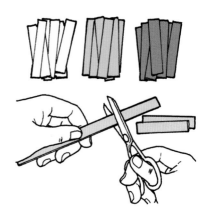

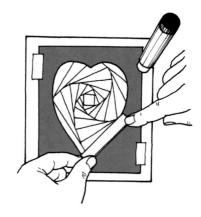

4 Cut the iris papers into 5cm (2in) strips. Group them together by colour and in the order you wish to use them.

5 Repeat steps 5–11 of the bauble on pages 48–49 with the four groups of coloured strips and silver square.

6 **To complete the heart**, remove the backing from the strips of double-sided tape on the back of the heart and mount it centrally on the red craft card. Place the silver sticky-backed gem heart in to the heart's centre.

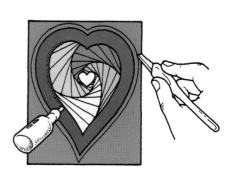

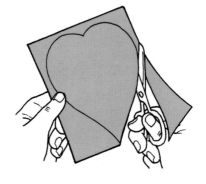

7 Echoing the heart's shape, trim the red craft card leaving a border of approximately 0.2cm (^{1}/$_{16}$in). Go around the inside edge of the heart's aperture with crystal glitter glue.

8 Trace the shadow heart template from page 115 and transfer it onto the rose patterned paper. Using the scissors, cut out the heart.

9 Glue the iris heart slightly over the shadow heart, as shown.

10 **To make a card**, apply glue to the back of the gold spider web paper, turn it lengthways on and mount it on the front of the black two-panel card, adjacent to the card's folded side. Glue the red ribbon over the web paper's right-hand side, as shown. Attach the craft bow to the ribbon, slightly below the ribbon's top edge.

11 Apply glue to the back of the hearts and mount them on the front of the two-panel card, slightly towards the card's right-hand side and bottom corner, as shown.

12 To finish, complete the decorations with magical-themed stickers and crystal glitter glue.

Anniversary gift box

you will need

6.5 x 8cm (2⁵/₈ x 3¹/₈in) rectangle of white pearlescent craft card

7 x 9cm (2¾ x 3½in) rectangle of gold craft card

Four 2 x 40cm (¾ x 15¾in) rectangles of pearlescent paper for the iris folds – one each in purple, gold, bronze and beige

2cm (¾in) square of silver paper

6.5 x 8.5cm (2⁵/₈ x 3³/₈in) rectangle of red pearlescent craft card

Purple sticky-backed gem heart

Crystal glitter glue

Adhesive foam pads

Basic tool kit

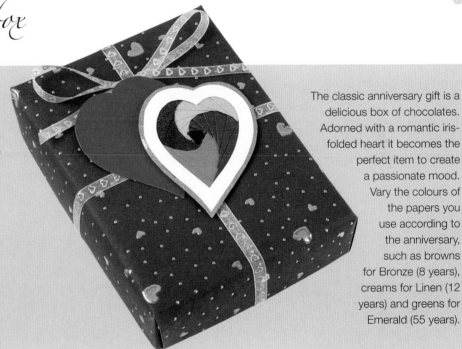

The classic anniversary gift is a delicious box of chocolates. Adorned with a romantic iris-folded heart it becomes the perfect item to create a passionate mood. Vary the colours of the papers you use according to the anniversary, such as browns for Bronze (8 years), creams for Linen (12 years) and greens for Emerald (55 years).

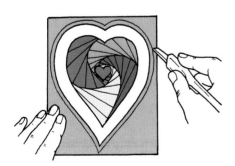

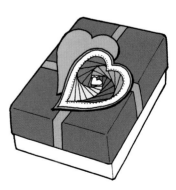

1 **To make the gift box decoration,** begin by repeating steps 1–7 of the heart on page 52 with the white pearlescent and gold craft cards, iris papers, silver square, purple sticky-backed gem and crystal glitter glue.

2 Trace the shadow heart template from page 115 and transfer it onto the red pearlescent craft card. Using the craft knife and cutting mat, cut out the heart. Glue the iris heart slightly over the shadow heart, as shown.

3 To finish, attach the joined hearts to your gift box with adhesive foam pads, so that they rise up slightly.

Scrapbook page

you will need

To decorate a scrapbook page approximately 30.5cm (12in) square

6.5 x 8cm (2⅝ x 3⅛in) rectangle of red pearlescent craft card

Four 2 x 35cm (¾ x 14in) rectangles of paper for the iris folds – one each in red textured, orange, pink and wine

2cm (¾in) square of silver paper

A5 (21 x 14.8cm / 8¼ x 5⅞in) rectangle of white pearlescent craft card

15.5 x 22cm (6⅛ x 8⅝in) rectangle of wine craft paper

10 x 15cm (4 x 6in) portrait-wise photograph (large)

9 x 10cm (3½ x 4in) portrait-wise photograph (small)

9 x 10cm (3½ x 4in) rectangle of rose patterned paper

Two 30.5cm (12in) lengths of 2cm (¾in) wide pink organza ribbon

30.5cm (12in) length of 1cm (⅜in) wide red tartan ribbon

Red sticky-backed gem heart

Themed stickers and embellishments such as bouquets, hearts, rings, bows and shoes

Basic tool kit

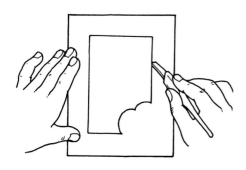

1 **To prepare**, trace the heart photo frame template from page 114 and transfer it onto the white pearlescent craft card. Using the craft knife, cutting mat and metal ruler, cut out the frame's aperture.

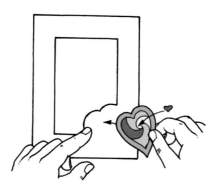

2 Repeat steps 1–5 of the heart on page 52 with the red pearlescent craft card, iris papers (cutting each one into 5cm (2in) strips) and silver square. Place the red sticky-backed gem heart in to the heart's centre. Remove the backing from the strips of double-sided tape on the back of the heart and mount it on the frame's bottom right-hand corner, as shown.

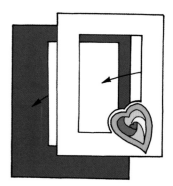

3 Position the frame centrally over the large photograph and glue firmly in place. Glue the framed photograph centrally on the wine craft paper.

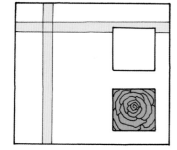

4 Decorate the scrapbook page with the lengths of organza ribbon, the small photograph and rose patterned paper. When you are satisfied with their positions, glue them in place.

5 Place the framed photograph on the page at an attractive angle. When you are satisfied with its position, glue it in place.

6 To finish, complete the decorations with the red tartan ribbon, themed stickers and embellishments.

Avoid the temptation to overload scrapbook pages with too many decorative items. In general the more you add the greater the chance that you will detract from the main theme. Your memorabilia should always dominate, with the other elements enhancing rather than detracting.

Iris-folded Frames

The soft edges of an iris-folded mount offer a refreshing change from the usual straight edge of a shop-bought picture frame. Choosing the paper colours and patterns, and the embellishments for your photo frame is a very personal thing, but you need to select the right colours to enhance your chosen photograph. You can design the frame to pick up colours in the pictures, or even incorporate small precious mementos into the iris aperture. Iris folding creates such an intriguing pattern of swirling papers that sometimes a simple frame is the best to show off the beauty of the papers and trimmings, without detracting from your photograph.

Pet photo frame

you will need

12cm (4¾in) square of jaguar print craft card

12.5cm (5in) square of black craft card

Four 2 x 42cm (¾ x 16½in) rectangles of paper for the iris folds – one each in brown, black, light brown and yellow

14 x 28cm (5½ x 11in) rectangle of mocha-brown craft card

7cm (2¾in) square photograph

Themed embellishments such as paw prints and bones

Basic tool kit

Child's photo frame

you will need

12cm (4¾in) square of blue pearlescent craft card

12.5cm (5in) square of white craft card

Four 2 x 42cm (¾ x 16½in) rectangles of paper for the iris folds – one each in blue, light blue, dark blue and metallic blue

14 x 28cm (5½ x 11in) rectangle of navy blue craft card

7cm (2¾in) square photograph

Themed embellishments such as clouds and boats

Basic tool kit

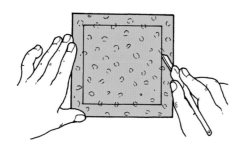

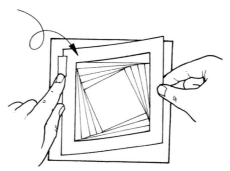

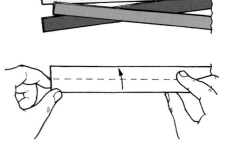

1 **To prepare**, trace the photo frame template from page 118 and transfer it onto the jaguar print craft card. Using the craft knife, cutting mat and metal ruler, cut out the frame's aperture.

2 Turn the aperture over and line it up with the folding pattern on page 118. Use small pieces of masking tape to hold the aperture in place on top of the pattern.

3 Place the iris papers sideways on, with their white side on top. Valley fold each one in half from bottom to top.

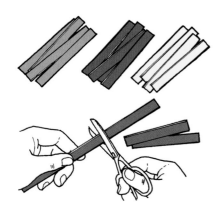

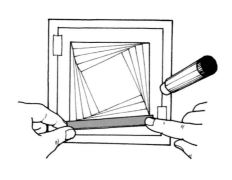

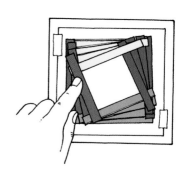

4 Cut the iris papers into 10.5cm (4¹⁄₈in) strips. Group them together by colour and in the order you wish to use them.

5 Repeat steps 5–7 of the bauble on page 48 with the four groups of coloured strips.

6 Continue working anti-clockwise around the folding pattern, taking a coloured strip from each of the groups in turn and making one full round each time.

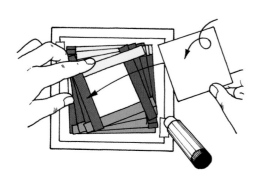

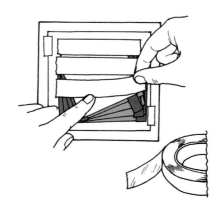

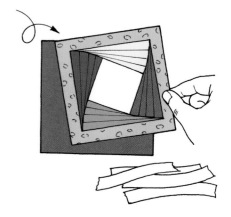

7 Turn the photograph face down and place it centrally over the iris folding. Glue it in place.

8 Apply double-sided tape to the back of the photograph and iris folding, as shown. Remove the aperture from the pattern.

9 Remove the backing from the strips of double-sided tape. Turn the aperture over and mount it centrally on the black craft card.

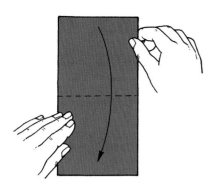

10 Turn the mocha-brown craft card lengthways on. Lightly score along its horizontal middle line, turn over and valley fold in half from top to bottom along the scored line.

11 Apply glue to the back of the photo frame and mount it centrally on the card's front surface.

12 Decorate around the aperture with themed embellishments. To finish, open out the card slightly so that it will stand up.

Child's photo frame
This frame, designed around a photo of a child, is created in exactly the same way as the pet photo frame – just using different papers and embellishments to match the theme of the photograph. You could also try out some other themes, such as a wedding photo frame using soft cream papers with horseshoe and flower embellishments, or a baby photo frame using pretty pastel papers with dummies and safety pin embellishments. What a better way to save a priceless moment than by creating something unique to be treasured forever?
Finished size of both frames:
14 x 14cm (5½ x 5½in)

Origami

People have been folding paper ever since it was invented in China in 105ce. However, it was in Japan, during the Edo period (1615–1868) when paper finally became inexpensive enough for everyone to use, that origami became a form of entertainment. The various ways of folding paper to make animals, flowers and other artefacts were passed down through many successive generations. Beginning in the 1890s, the Japanese government established a widespread system of pre-school education, and origami was introduced as a tool for co-ordinating young minds and hands. Since the 1950s, interest has grown in Britain, the United States and Europe, as well as in Japan. Origami is as intriguing to adults as it is to children, and there are challenges to be had at all levels of expertise. Moreover, you will discover the magic in transforming a flat piece of paper into a three-dimensional work of art.

TOOLS

Paper
Any paper that takes a fold well can be used for origami. Using a thinner paper makes the folding process easier, more satisfying and the end result a lot more pleasing. Part of the folding process involves deciding which pattern or colour will look best with which model. Packaged origami paper is readily available in a wide range of colours, patterns, textures and sizes; occasionally you may find packs containing only one colour. For practising an origami model, it is usually best to start with a 15cm (6in) square. Of course, you can always cut your own squares from coloured photocopying paper, writing paper, gift wrap or any reasonably thin paper, making sure they are cut absolutely square. There is nothing more frustrating than trying to fold paper that is not quite square. The paper you use doesn't have to be coloured on one side, although this helps to make the completed model look more attractive.

Folding equipment
Origami is unique among paper crafts in that it really requires no tools other than paper itself and the most basic of equipment – your own two hands. The flat surface of your fingernail is a great folding aid, even better for making neat folds than the edge of your nail. However, if you prefer to use a folding tool to sharpen your folds, purchase a bone folder, or use a less expensive alternative such as a butter knife or an old credit card. A flat, clean tabletop or large hard-backed book makes the ideal surface to fold upon.

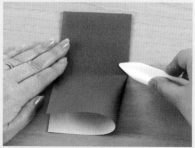

TECHNIQUES

Jewellery making
Completed origami models are easily transformed into unique wearable jewellery. Findings (such as necklace clasps, brooch backs and earring wires) can be purchased in a craft or jewellery store. To make earrings thread a needle with a length of beading thread, and add on beads and your origami shapes. To prevent beads from falling off, tie a double knot at the end of the thread. Attach a silver earring wire onto the thread. Tighten it against the beads with a double knot, and trim off any excess thread. For a necklace, again thread the needle with beading thread. Attach a silver barrel clasp at one end of the thread with a double knot. Add on your origami shapes and tie the thread's free end to the other end of the clasp with a double knot. To finish trim off any excess threads.

Toshie's Yacht

Origami is an extremely inexpensive way of creating interesting embellishments for card making. This yacht was originally taught to us by its creator, our friend the late Toshie Takahama of Tokyo, Japan. It only takes a few folds of paper to make a very attractive model.

you will need

12cm (4¾in) square of origami paper

Basic tool kit

Yacht card

For a greetings card, attach a rectangle of silver craft fabric net to the bottom of a light blue two-panel card. Glue the yacht on top. Nautical and sea-themed peel-off stickers make an ideal finishing touch.

Finished size of card: 21 x 14.8cm (8¼ x 5⅞in)

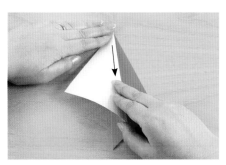

1 Turn the square of origami paper around to look like a diamond, with the white side on top. Fold and unfold in half from right to left. From the top corner, valley fold the right-hand sloping edge in to meet the middle fold-line.

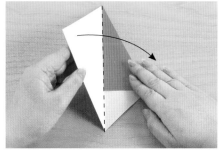

2 Valley fold the left-hand flap of paper over to the right.

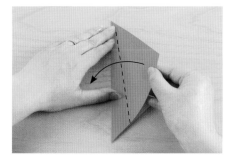

3 Starting slightly short of the top corner…

4 … valley fold the flap of paper back over to the left on a slant, making a sail.

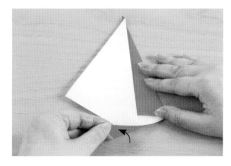

5 Valley fold the bottom point over on a slant, making the keel.

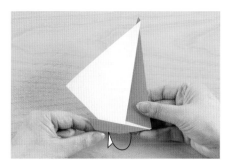

6 To finish, mountain fold a little of the keel's bottom point behind itself so giving the yacht a flat bottom.

Five-pointed Star

While the folding steps of this model might seem very easy, do not be fooled. They are simple, but like many other paperfolded projects the more carefully you make the initial folds, the neater the end result will be. Origami models can quickly be transformed into paper jewellery. You can make earrings, bracelets and necklaces bold or delicate and in all colours of the rainbow to match or contrast with any style of clothing.

Jewellery set

you will need

Needle with a large eye

Beading thread

Basic tool kit

For a pair of earrings

Six 1 x 20cm (3/8 x 8in) rectangles of pearlescent paper – two each in white, light blue and dark blue

Two 0.3cm (1/8in) pearl beads

Two 0.5cm (1/4in) blue beads

Two silver earring wires with hooks

For a necklace

Thirty 1 x 20cm (3/8 x 8in) rectangles of pearlescent paper –six each in light blue and dark blue and eighteen in white

Silver barrel clasp

For a bracelet

Fifteen 1 x 20cm (3/8 x 8in) rectangles of pearlescent paper – three each in light blue and dark blue and nine in white

Spandex elastic

Star earrings
When made on this small scale, the five-pointed star can be used as a form of paper bead for use in creative jewellery making. These charming earrings can be made in any colour variations you desire, to compliment a favourite outfit. See page 65 for project instructions.

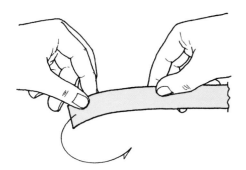

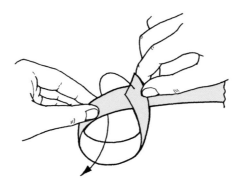

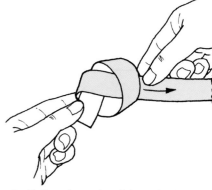

1 **To make a five-pointed star**, turn one rectangle of pearlescent paper sideways on, with the coloured side on top. Make an overhand loop at the left-hand end.

2 Tuck the working end through the loop already formed.

3 Pull on the end to tighten the knot. Flatten the knot into the shape of a regular pentagon. Adjust the short and long ends accordingly.

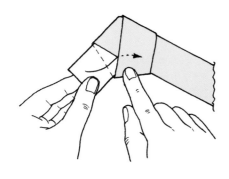

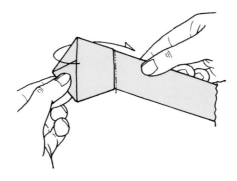

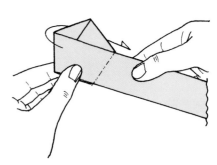

4 Tuck the short end inside the knot. The end should not protrude past the knot. If it does, cut or fold it a little shorter.

5 With a mountain fold, wrap one side of the knot around the long end, as shown.

6 Again, wrap the knot around the long end and towards an opposite side.

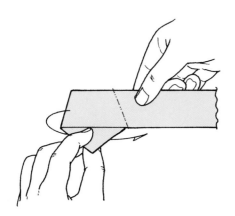

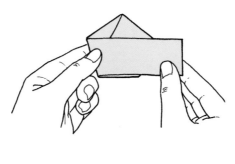

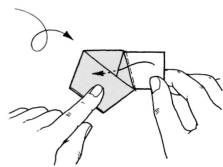

7 Continue wrapping the knot around the long end in a way that keeps the regular pentagon shape.

8 As you wrap around the knot, make the folds as tight as possible.

9 Turn the knot over. Finally, tuck the free end into the knot, making a multi-layer knot. If the end is a too long, cut a little off and then tuck it inside.

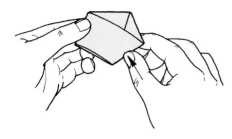

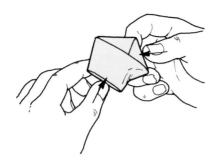

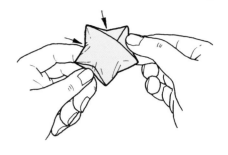

10 Hold the knot between two fingers at the side edges, as shown. With your other hand, push in gently with your thumbnail the middle of one side, causing it to indent inwards slightly.

11 Repeat step 10 on the remaining four sides, making the knot become three-dimensional.

12 The completed five-pointed star.

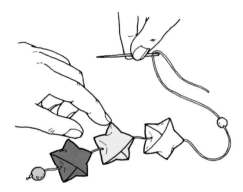

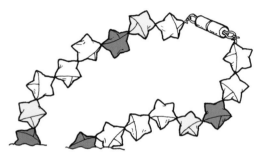

13 **For a pair of earrings**, thread the needle with a 30.5cm (12in) length of beading thread. Add on a blue bead and to prevent it from falling off, tie a double knot at the end of the thread. Add on three five-pointed stars, varying the colours as you go, and a pearl bead.

14 Attach a silver earring wire on to the thread. Tighten it against the pearl bead with a double knot. To finish, trim off any excess thread. Repeat steps 13 and 14 to make another earring.

15 **For a necklace**, thread the needle with a little over 60cm (24in) of beading thread. Attach a silver barrel clasp at one end of the thread with a double knot. Add on thirty five-pointed stars, varying the colours as you go. Tie the thread's free end to the other end of the clasp with a double knot. To finish, trim off any excess thread.

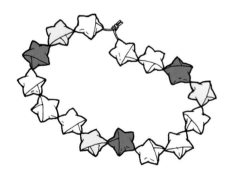

16 **For a bracelet**, measure a length of spandex elastic to fit comfortably around your wrist and then allow a little extra. Add on fifteen five-pointed stars, varying the colours as you go. Tie the ends of the elastic together in a double knot. To finish, trim off any excess elastic.

Varying the colour of the paper can create a totally different mood to the jewellery for different occasions. You could make a set to wear to a wedding to co-ordinate with the bride's dress, or give a set to a friend in their favourite colours. The elastic used in the bracelet means that it should fit any wrist comfortably.

Hina Dolls

Hinamatsuri (Dolls' festival) is celebrated on 3 March in Japan. Most Japanese families with girls display a set of elaborate dolls called *hina ningyo* dressed in the many-layered costumes of the Heian court (794–1185). The dolls are usually arranged on a five or seven-tiered stand covered with red material. The Emperor and Empress are seated on the top tier (backed by a decorative gold screen), followed by ladies in waiting, musicians, ministers and servants. There are also ceremonial trays, saké sets, tea sets, chests for clothing and miniature mandarin orange and peach trees. Many young Japanese girls invite their friends over to help celebrate the festival and fold Hina dolls from squares of paper, using them to decorate invitation cards.

Pop-up card

you will need

Two 12cm (4¾in) squares of flower-patterned paper – one each in blue and pink

A5 (21 x 14.8cm/8¼ x 5⅞in) rectangle of red craft card

A5 (21 x 14.8cm/8¼ x 5⅞in) rectangle of red craft paper

6.5 x 13cm (2⅝ x 5in) rectangle of gold craft paper

Two 6 x 0.8cm (2⅜ x 5/16in) rectangles of multi-coloured striped paper

5 x 15cm (2 x 6in) rectangle of pink pearlescent craft paper

Black felt-tip pen

Flower punch

Basic tool kit

Doll designs

Super place cards can be made from an 8 x 15cm (3⅛ x 6in) rectangle of red craft card, which is mountain folded in half lengthways and decorated with a Hina doll folded from a 10cm (4in) square of paper. The bookmarks shown in the photo opposite are made from a 5 x 17cm (2 x 6¾in) rectangle of pearlescent craft card, decorated with Hina dolls folded from 7.5cm (3in) squares of paper and adorned with multi-coloured punched flowers.

Finished size of place cards: 6 x 15cm (2⅜ x 6in)
Finished size of pop-up card: 10.5 x 14.8cm (4⅛ x 5⅞in)
Finished size of bookmarks: 17 x 5cm (6¾ x 2in)

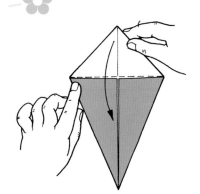 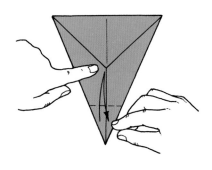 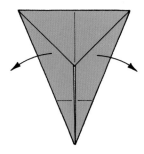

1 **To make the Emperor,** begin by repeating steps 1 and 2 for the rosette on page 20 with the square of blue flower-patterned paper. Valley fold the kite base's top point down along the horizontal edges, making a triangle.

2 Valley fold the bottom point up to meet the triangle's tip. Press flat and unfold it.

3 Unfold the edges from underneath the triangle.

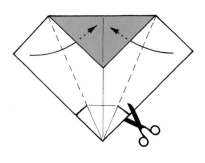 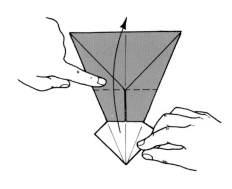 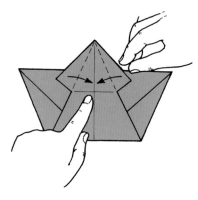

4 From either side of the bottom point, cut along the two short sloping fold-lines, as far as shown. From above the cuts, valley fold the sloping edges in to meet the middle fold-line, while at the same time tucking them underneath the triangle.

5 Valley fold the bottom point up along a horizontal line that runs adjacent to the triangle's tip.

6 Valley fold the middle point's sloping edges in to meet the adjacent vertical fold-line, making the Emperor's face.

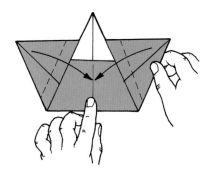 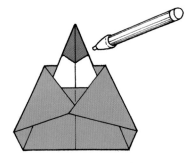 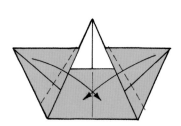

7 Valley fold the left-hand point over on a slant towards the Emperor's lap, making his right shoulder and sleeve. Repeat with the right-hand point, so that it lies on top.

8 To finish, draw on and colour in the Emperor's V-shaped hairline and hat with the black felt-tip pen, as shown.

9 **To make the Empress,** begin by repeating steps 1–6 of the Emperor with the square of pink flower-patterned paper. Repeat step 7, but making her shoulders slightly narrower than those of the Emperor.

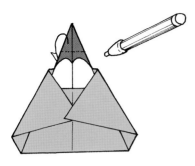

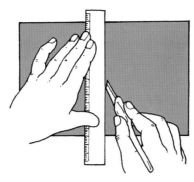

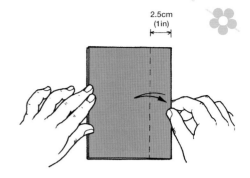

10 Drawn on and colour in the Empress's M-shaped hairline with the black felt-tip pen, as shown. To finish, shape the Empress's head by mountain folding a little of the top point behind itself. Glue it down.

11 **To make a card**, turn the red craft card sideways on. Lightly score down its vertical middle line, turn over and valley fold in half from right to left along the scored line.

12 Valley fold in 2.5cm (1in) of the right hand side. Press flat and unfold it. Open out the paper from left to right.

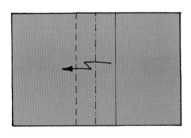

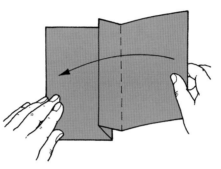

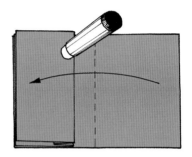

13 Along the fold-lines made in step 12, pleat the left-hand section of paper and then …

14 … valley fold the right-hand section of paper over to lie on top.

15 Apply glue to the back of the pleated paper and mount it on the craft card, adjacent to the card's left-hand side, at the same time aligning their top and bottom edges. Then apply glue to the front of the pleated paper. Along the scored line, valley fold the craft card in half from right to left. Press firmly so gluing the card and paper together.

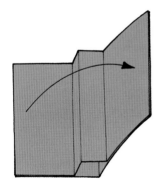

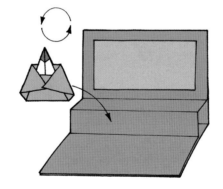

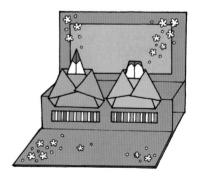

16 You have now made a two-panel card with a pleat on the inside. Make sure that the card opens and closes easily and the pleat rises up into a step.

17 Open out the card. Apply glue to the back of the gold craft paper, turn it sideways on and mount it centrally on the card's upper surface. Apply glue to the back of the Emperor adjacent to his bottom edge and mount him on the front of the step while making sure that he is positioned slightly below the top edge and towards the left-hand side.

18 Repeat step 19 with the Empress, gluing her towards the right-hand side. Apply glue to the back of the rectangles of striped paper, turn them sideways on and mount them underneath the dolls. Using the flower punch, punch flowers from the pink pearlescent craft paper. To finish, glue the flowers attractively around the card, as shown.

Celebration Cranes

This most famous of origami folds is often used throughout the world as a symbol of peace. If you fold a thousand cranes (*senbazuru*) within a year and thread them together, it is said that they will bring you long life and good fortune. Nowadays, it is a custom among Japanese children to make a garland of cranes from coloured squares of paper for friends who are ill, to wish them a speedy recovery. When folded from red and gold paper the fantail crane created by the late Toshio Chino has a refined simplicity that makes it the perfect embellishment to any wedding present, providing the wish for the couple to enjoy a long life and happy marriage. This exquisite fold will also make the ideal place card for special parties.

Crane

you will need

15cm (6in) square of red or white origami paper

Basic tool kit

Classic and fantail cranes
The classic crane design can be enhanced by the addition of a spectacular gold fantail. The use of duo paper makes this colour transition possible. The folding technique begins in the same way for both designs, but there are crucial differences as the model progresses. See project instructions on page 72 and page 76.

The cool stylings of the Far East take shape in compact crane chopstick rests that are perfect for any celebratory place setting. A 12cm (4¾in) square of origami paper makes the perfect chopstick rest.

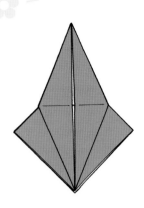

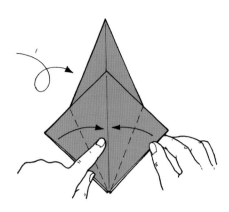

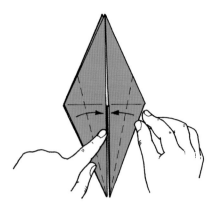

1 **To make a crane,** begin by repeating steps 1–8 for the floret on page 28 with the square of origami paper.

2 Turn the paper over. Repeat steps 3–8 for the floret on page 28. Press the paper flat, making a bird base.

3 Making sure that the split in the bird base is pointing towards you, valley fold the lower sloping edges (top layer only) in to lie …

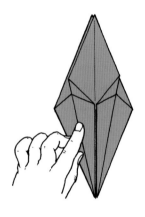

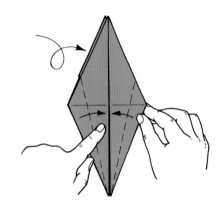

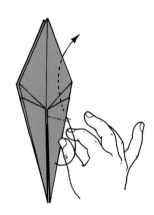

4 … slightly short of the vertical middle line.

5 Turn the paper over. Repeat steps 3 and 4.

6 Make the crane's head and tail by inside reverse folding the bottom points. This is what you do: place your forefinger into the groove of a bottom point and …

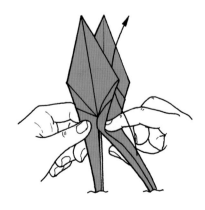

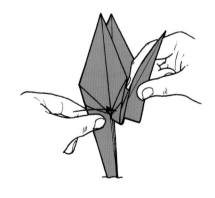

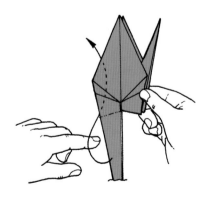

7 … with your thumb underneath, push the point up …

8 … inside itself, as shown. To complete, press the paper flat.

9 Repeat steps 6–8 with the remaining bottom point.

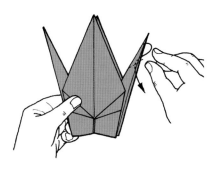

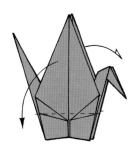

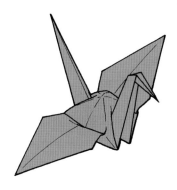

10 Inside reverse fold the tip of one of the top points to make the crane's head and beak.

11 Take hold of a wing in each hand and gently pull them apart …

12 … flattening out the middle point a little. This completes the crane.

Crane earrings

you will need

Two 7.5cm (3in) squares of orange pearlescent paper

Ten 0.3cm (¹/₈in) pearl beads

Two 0.5cm (¼in) pink beads

Long needle

Beading thread

Two silver ear wires with hooks

Basic tool kit

1 **To make a pair of earrings**, begin by repeating steps 1–12 for the crane with the one square of orange pearlescent paper. Thread the needle with a 30.5cm (12in) length of beading thread. Add on a 0.5cm (¼in) bead.

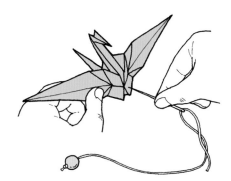

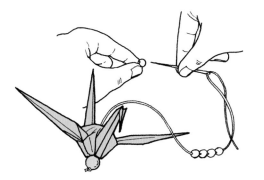

2 To prevent the bead from falling off, tie a double knot at the end of the thread. Add on the crane by inserting the needle through the small hole that you will find at the bottom of the crane.

3 Add on five 0.3cm (¹/₈in) beads.

4 Attach a silver ear wire onto the thread. Tighten it against the bead with a double knot. To finish, trim off any excess thread. Repeat steps 1–4 to make another earring.

Senbazuru

you will need

One thousand 7.5cm (3in) squares of origami paper in a variety of colours

15cm (6in) square of gold origami paper

Forty 7.5cm (3in) squares of origami paper – twenty each in red and black

Red wooden bead with a large centre hole

Long needle

Beading thread

Gold thread

Basic tool kit

One of the most moving examples of *senbazuru* used as a prayer for peace can be seen at the Peace Park in Hiroshima, Japan. There, stands a statue of a young girl holding in her hands, high in the air, a metal sculptured crane and hanging from it are many thousands of origami cranes made by visitors from all over the world.

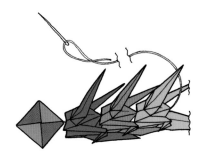

1 **To make a *senbazuru*,** begin by repeating steps 1–12 for the crane with the square of gold origami paper and steps 1–10 with the one thousand squares of origami paper. A little patience and perseverance will serve you well during the folding of the cranes.

2 Repeat steps 1–6 of the coaster on page 93 with the forty squares of red and black paper, making twenty coasters.

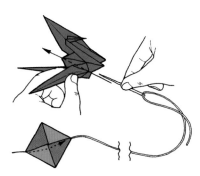

3 **To assemble,** thread the needle with a little over 1m (39¼in) of beading thread. Add on a coaster and to prevent it from falling off, tie a very large knot at the end of the thread. Add on a crane by inserting the needle through the small hole that you will find at the bottom of the crane.

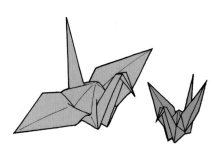

4 Add on forty-nine more cranes, either all of the same colour or in a variety of colours. Tighten the cranes against each other as your work. This completes one strand of the *senbazuru*.

5 Repeat steps 3 and 4 with the remaining cranes and coasters, making a further nineteen strands. Thread the needle with a doubled length of gold thread. Gather the *senbazuru* strands up and along with the gold thread's free ends, tie them **all** together in a double knot. Pass the thread through the wooden bead's centre hole, slipping the bead over the knot. Trim off any protruding threads.

6 Add on the golden crane by inserting the needle through the small hole that you will find at the bottom of the crane. Cut the needle free and tie the thread's ends together in a double knot. To finish, push the crane down the thread, so that it comes to rest on top of the bead.

Fantail crane

you will need

15cm (6in) square of red and gold
duo paper

Basic tool kit

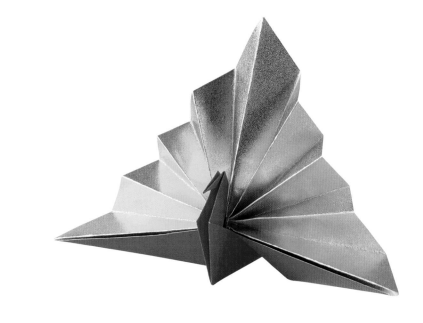

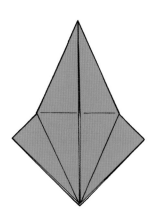

1 Begin by repeating steps 1–8 for the floret on page 28 with the square of duo paper, but with the gold side on top in step 1.

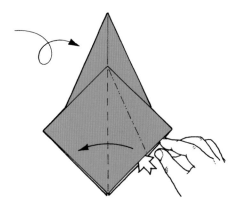

2 Turn the paper over. Open out the right hand flap and press it down neatly in a diamond shape.

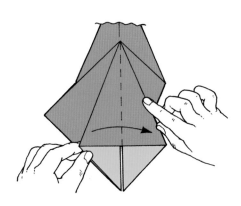

3 Valley fold the diamond in half from left to right, like turning a page of a book.

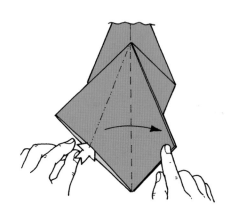

4 Open out the left-hand flap and press it down neatly in a diamond shape.

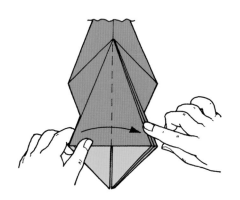

5 Repeat step 3.

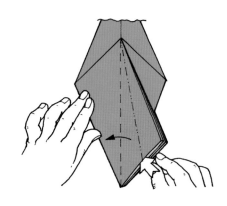

6 Open out and press down neatly one right-hand flap, as shown.

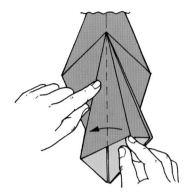

7 Valley fold the flap in half from right to left.

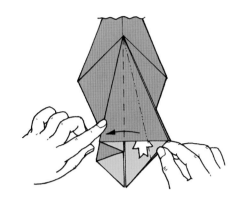

8 Repeat steps 6 and 7 with the remaining three right-hand flaps.

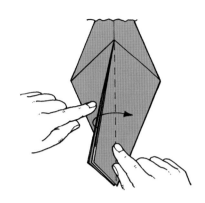

9 Valley fold four left-hand layers over to the right, making the tail.

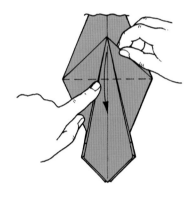

10 Valley fold the middle point down on a line between the two side points, as shown.

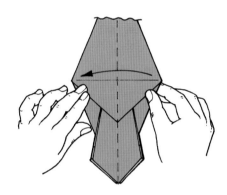

11 Valley fold the paper in half from right to left.

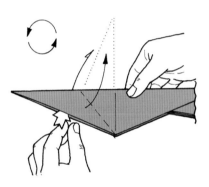

12 Turn the paper around so that the tail points towards the right. Outside reverse fold the left-hand point into the position shown by the dotted lines.

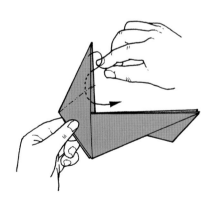

13 Inside reverse fold the left-hand point down to lie along the tail's top edge.

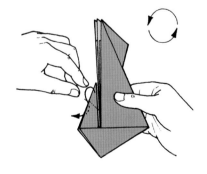

14 Turn the paper around into the position shown. Inside reverse fold the left-hand point's tip, making the head and beak.

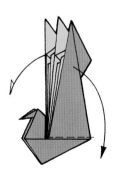

15 To finish, open out the tail and arrange its folds into a fan-like shape.

Tissue Folding

The use of tissue paper as a source of foldable material is
sometimes overlooked. So often this type of paper is taken
for granted and, although regularly used as gift wrapping material, it is
seldom that one thinks of pleating it decoratively or of using just a few twists and
curls to produce breathtaking flowers that encapsulate all the grace and beauty of their
real-life models. Paper flowers are a recognized part of Mexican tradition. The craft of making
paper flowers was originally brought to Mexico from East Asia – which is why the tissue used to
make them, is called 'papel de China'. In Japan, paper flowers and other decorations are made
by children to celebrate *Tanabata*, the Star Festival, held on the evening of 7 July. Tissue-folded
flowers are just right for adding colour and visual interest to your life, from arrangements for the
home, to bouquets and corsages.

TOOLS

Paper
Tissue paper is lightweight but strong and comes in a
wide range of colours including metallics. Good-quality
paper has a sheen on its surface. A special quality to be
discovered in tissue is the intensity of colour, which is
enriched when several layers are placed together. Iron
out any creases, but **only** use a very **cold** iron setting.
Take care not to get tissue paper wet; even a few drops
of water can cause the dye to run and spoil the paper.
Be careful how you handle tissue paper when gluing, as
it can be stretched easily with a glue stick and soak up
wet glue, becoming hard to handle.

Floristry supplies
The most essential item for tissue flowers, apart from the paper, is
the florists' wire, which you will need to give the flower its support
and structure. This can be obtained from florists, art and craft stores.
It is available in a large range of gauges and pre-cut lengths and can
be obtained either uncovered or covered with paper (usually green
or white). For the following projects a 20-gauge wire is ideal. A small
pair of pliers is essential for cutting and bending the wire. Floral tape
is used to fasten flowers onto florists' wire, and to bind the wires
so they look more like real flower stems. The tape is made from a
crepe-like material, impregnated with adhesive, and is available in
a large range of colours, including brown, green and white. Oasis
is plastic foam used
as a base for floral
arrangements. It
comes in various
shapes and sizes
and can be cut
easily with a knife.

Tissue Tulips

Try this sample project to practise and perfect tissue folding, before progressing to the following projects. The exquisite tulip, with its long and elegant stem will add a certain kind of beauty to any room. Make the flower in a variety of colours for a stunning arrangement. Try to make the folds soft and gently in order not to tear the paper.

you will need

For one tulip

5 x 12cm (2 x 4¾in) rectangle of tulip-coloured tissue paper such as orange, pink, red or yellow

21cm (8¼in) length of 20-gauge green covered florists' wire

Green floral tape

Basic tool kit

Tulip bouquet
Make a few more tulips and tie them together with a decorative ribbon bow to form a bouquet.

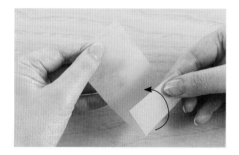

1 **To make a tulip**, place the rectangle of tissue paper sideways on. Loosely roll the right-hand side towards the left.

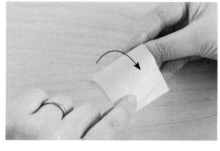

2 Continue to loosely roll the tissue paper, making it tube-like.

3 Using the pliers, bend a small hook into one end of the florists' wire. Insert the wire's hooked end in to the bottom of the tube.

4 Pinch the bottom of the tube and wire together. Carefully arrange the tube's layers to suggest the tulip's closed bell-like flower head.

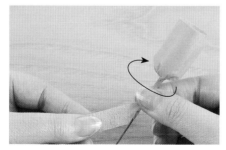

5 Gently stretch a length of green floral tape to release the impregnated adhesive. Wrap the tape around the base of the tulip a few times, fastening it onto the florists' wire.

6 To finish, slant the tape at a downward angle and wind it spirally down, covering the wire by rotating the tulip.

Small Buds

If flowers are the language of love, then let them burst forth. Flowers are a symbol of rejoicing and they can transform the plainest of items into a fantasia of colour. Small paper buds encapsulate all the grace and beauty of their real-life counterparts. They require a little patience if you wish to make many of them – but the results are stunning. There are more elaborate artistic methods to create paper flowers, but the following flower is just perfect for adding a splash of vibrant colour to any greetings card.

Small buds card

you will need

Dark brown two-panel card

Seven 7cm (2¾in) squares of white tissue paper

10cm (4in) square of white craft card

9cm (3½in) square of white spider web paper

48cm (19in) length of 1.2cm (½in) wide white ribbon

Four pearl gems

White craft bow with a pearl centre

Two pink hearts each with a 6cm (2³/₈in) length of silver thread

Six turquoise green leaf stickers

Crystal glitter glue

Basic tool kit

Pink buds card
A sumptuous selection of pink buds all beautifully arranged on a white embossed card. By all means aim to copy the buds exactly as they appear in the photograph, but do remember that no two artists are alike. What is important is your own personal touch – the feelings and life that you inject into your work. See page 83 for project instructions.
Finished size of both cards: 21 x 14.8cm (8¼ x 5⅞in)

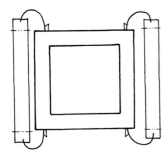

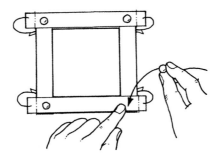

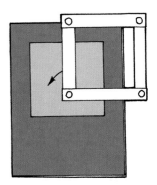

1 **To prepare**, trace the small buds card frame template from page 117 and transfer it onto the white craft card. Using the craft knife, cutting mat and metal ruler, cut out the card's aperture. Cut the white ribbon into four 12cm (4¾in) lengths. Glue two lengths of ribbon to the sides of the frame so their ends protrude slightly. Mountain fold the ends behind the frame and glue them down.

2 Glue the remaining lengths of ribbon to the top and bottom of the frame so their ends protrude slightly. Mountain fold the ends behind the frame and glue them down. Decorate with the pearl gems; gluing one in each corner of the frame.

3 Apply glue to the back of the white spider web paper and mount it on the front of the dark brown two-panel card, slightly below the card's top edge, as shown. Apply glue to the back of the frame and mount it centrally on the web paper.

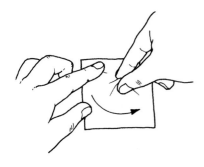

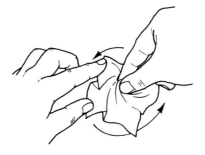

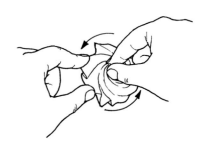

4 **To make a bud**, place one square of white tissue paper on your working surface. Pinch the middle with the finger and thumb of one hand. Twist the tissue paper anti-clockwise around the middle with your free hand.

5 Arrange the tissue paper into neat furrows with the fingers of your free hand, while still holding the middle and continuing to twist anti-clockwise.

6 Keep on twisting until you can twist no further.

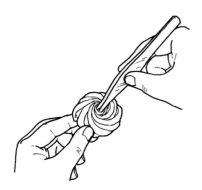

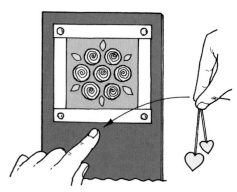

7 Holding the tissue paper by its lower edges and using a pair of tweezers, tightly twist the middle furrows, making a tight bud. Tuck any protruding edges of paper underneath the bud. Repeat steps 4–7 with the remaining six squares of tissue paper.

8 Arrange the buds inside the aperture so that they are tightly packed together. When you are satisfied with the arrangement, glue them onto the spider web paper. Go around the buds' furrows with crystal glitter glue.

9 Attach the leaf stickers into the arrangement. Glue the pink hearts by the ends of their silver thread to the frame's bottom edge, as shown. To finish, glue the white craft bow on top of the ends of silver thread.

Pink buds card

you will need

Reddish brown two-panel card

Seven 7cm (2¾in) squares of pink tissue paper

14 x 20cm (5½ x 8in) rectangle of white embossed craft card

8 x 16cm (3⅛ x 6¼in) rectangle of white pearlescent paper

Pack of white and gold peel-off strips

Two white and gold peel-off trellises

White craft bow with a pearl centre

Small pink heart sticker

Two dark green leaf stickers

Crystal glitter glue

Basic tool kit

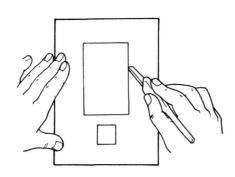

1 **To prepare**, trace the pink buds card window template from page 116 and transfer it onto the white embossed craft card. Using the craft knife, cutting mat and metal ruler, cut out the card's apertures.

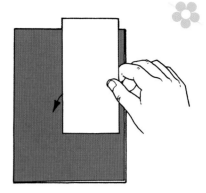

2 Apply glue to the back of the white pearlescent paper, turn it lengthways on and mount it centrally on the front of the reddish brown two-panel card.

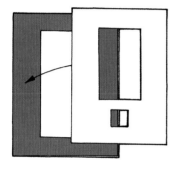

3 Apply glue to the back of the small buds window card, turn it lengthways on and mount it centrally on the front of the two-panel card.

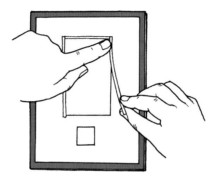

4 Attach white and gold peel-off strips along the sides and edges of both apertures, cutting off and discarding any excess.

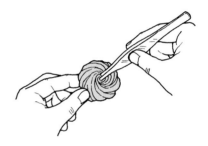

5 Repeat steps 4–7 of the small buds card with the squares of pink tissue paper.

6 Arrange the buds inside the large aperture so that they are tightly packed together. When you are satisfied with the arrangement, glue them onto the pearlescent paper. Position the leaf stickers into the arrangement, as shown.

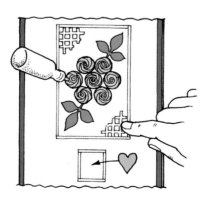

7 Go around the buds' furrows with crystal glitter glue. Attach the white and gold peel-off trellises to the large aperture's top left and bottom right-hand corners, as shown. Remove the backing from the heart sticker and attach it inside the small aperture.

8 To finish, glue the white craft bow to the large aperture's bottom edge, as shown.

Carnations

Paper carnations made from good-quality tissue paper are among some of the easiest and most attractive flowers to make. A pink carnation is the flower for Mother's Day, symbolizing 'always on my mind', red is for passion, white for sweet, lovely and good luck, but beware, striped carnations represent a refusal. A tissue-folded carnation makes an ideal table decoration as well as a place card for a birthday party. The flower can then be used as a buttonhole by the guests and taken home as a delightful souvenir of the occasion. Alternatively, fasten the flower to a circle of elastic, which can be worn around the wrist as a pompom bracelet.

Pink carnation

you will need

Eight 14 x 19cm (5½ x 7½in) rectangles of pale pink tissue paper

Plastic wire tie

Elastic fabric band that will fit loosely around your wrist

Basic tool kit

Yellow carnation
Exquisitely folded paper carnations can be made in any colour and be used for any number of decorative purposes. You can simply present them on their own, as part of an arrangement, or use them as a buttonhole or corsage. Leaves can easily be added for extra detail. See page 87 for project instructions.

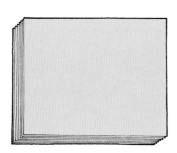

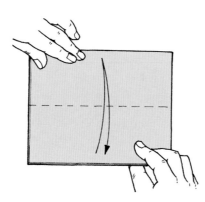

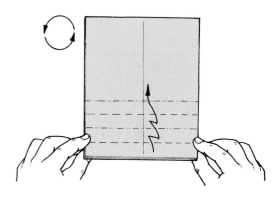

1 **To make a pink carnation**, turn the rectangles of pale pink tissue paper sideways on. Stack them together.

2 From now onwards treat **all** the rectangles of tissue paper as if they were one. Valley fold in half from bottom to top. Press flat and unfold.

3 Turn the tissue paper lengthways on. From the bottom edge, start to pleat the paper forwards and backwards in 1cm (3/8in) wide bands, as shown.

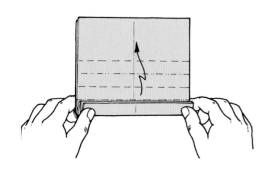

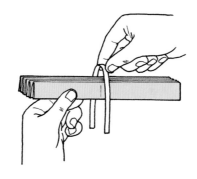

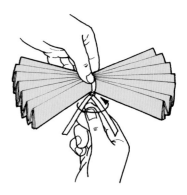

4 Take care with your pleating, and make sure that your folding is neat, with pleats falling one over the other. The end result should be a pleated strip of tissue paper, rather like a closed fan.

5 Bend the plastic wire tie into a loop and slip it around the middle of the pleats.

6 Tightly twist the ends of the wire tie together so holding the pleats in place.

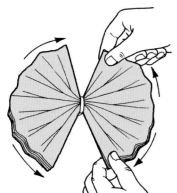

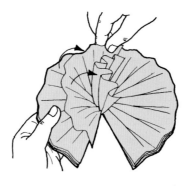

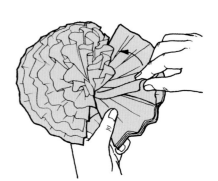

7 Fan out the pleats on either side of the wired middle.

8 Working with the left-hand pleats separate the top layer of tissue paper and make it stand upright by pulling it gently towards the wired middle. Repeat with each layer, taking great care not to tear the paper.

9 Repeat step 8 with the right-hand pleats.

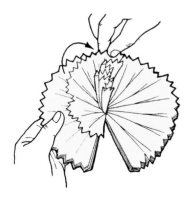

10 To finish, gently even out the carnation's layers.

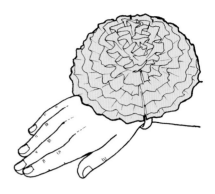

11 **For a bracelet**, place the wire tie's free ends around an elastic fabric band and twist them tightly together.

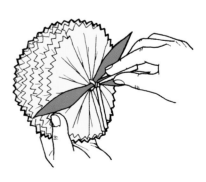

12 The completed bracelet worn on the wrist as a pompom.

Yellow carnation

you will need

Eight 10 x 14cm (4 x 5½in) rectangles of yellow tissue paper

6 x 12cm (2³/₈ x 4³/₄in) rectangle of green craft paper

Plastic wire tie

Deckle-edged scissors

Basic tool kit

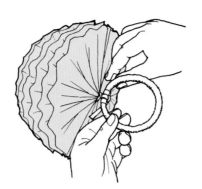

1 **To make a yellow carnation**, begin by repeating steps 1–7 of the pink carnation with the rectangles of yellow tissue paper and plastic wire tie.

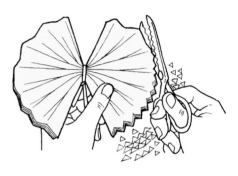

2 Fan out the pleats on either side of the wired middle. Using the deckle-edged scissors, trim the edges of the pleats, as shown.

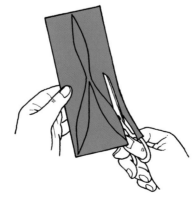

3 Repeat steps 8 and 9 of the pink carnation, taking great care not to tear the layers of tissue paper.

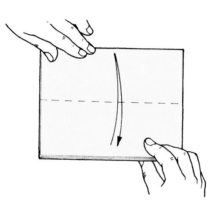

4 **To make a leaf**, trace the carnation leaf template from page 117 and transfer it onto the green craft paper. Using the scissors, cut out the leaf.

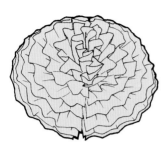

5 To finish, place the wire tie's free ends around the leaf's middle and twist them tightly together.

TISSUE FOLDING   87

Paper Roses

Although they are not as fragrant as real roses, paper roses will last for more than a day. A single red rose can give a romantic touch to a gift, or indeed be a gift in itself, while a larger arrangement of roses will make a beautiful and unusual bridal, or evening, bouquet or can be used to decorate a larger box. Sending flowers must be one of the most special ways to brighten up someone's day. The roses that follow have been adapted from a 1920s ribbon trim accessory.

Single rose box

you will need

5 x 70cm (2 x 27½in) rectangle of red tissue paper

4.5 x 10cm (1¾ x 4in) rectangle of green craft paper

7cm (2¾in) square gift box

Basic tool kit

What could be more romantic and glamorous than a ring box decorated with a large red rose? This is a gift that is sure to express your feelings to a loved one in a unique and thoughtful way. See what message you can create with the language of flowers (see box on page 90). After all, the rose is not only symbolic of love …

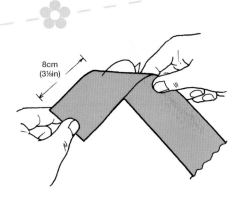

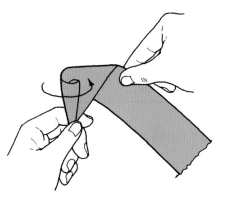

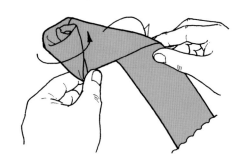

1 **To make the single rose box**, place the rectangle of red tissue paper sideways on. Make a soft sloping mountain fold at a point that is 8cm (3⅛in) away from the left-hand side, as shown.

2 Loosely roll the left-hand side over on itself, making the stem.

3 Softly mountain fold the right-hand section of tissue paper while rolling the stem along the fold.

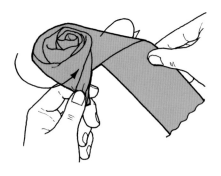

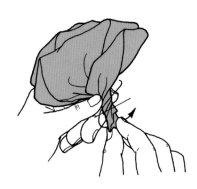

4 Continue on making a soft mountain fold and rolling the stem along the fold. You are creating the rose's petals.

5 Repeat step 4 until you reach the end of the tissue paper.

6 Tightly twist the stem's layers together. Cut the stem at a point 1cm (³⁄₈in) down from the base of the rose.

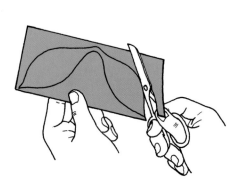

7 **To make a leaf**, trace the rose leaf A template from page 117 and transfer it onto the green craft paper. Using the scissors, cut out the leaf.

8 To finish, using double-sided tape, attach the leaf centrally to the lid of your gift box and the rose above.

The language of flowers
You can make your gift extra special if the flower's colour sends a send a message too. Here are a few of the more traditional meanings of rose colours. You could also include in a bouquet of roses a card that explains the precise meaning of each colour.

White – innocence, purity and charm

Red – love and passion

Pink – admiration, grace and thanks

Orange – enthusiasm and desire

Gold – the pinnacle of achievement

Bouquet of roses

1 **To make a bouquet**, using the pliers, bend a small hook into one end of a length of florists' wire. Place one long rectangle of beige pearlescent tissue paper sideways on. Make a soft sloping mountain fold at a point that is 8cm (3¹/₈in) away from the left-hand side and place the hooked wire on top, as shown.

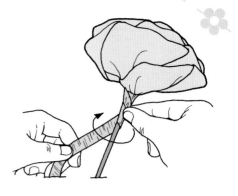

2 Repeat steps 2–5 of the single rose box. Tape around the base of the rose, fastening it onto the florists' wire. To finish, continue taping to the end of the wire. Make a further ten roses.

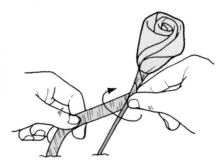

3 **To make a bud**, begin by repeating step 1 of the bouquet with a length of florists' wire and one short rectangle of beige pearlescent tissue paper. Repeat steps 2–5 of the single rose box. Tape around the base of the bud, fastening it onto the florist's wire. To finish, continue taping to the end of the wire. Make a further seven buds.

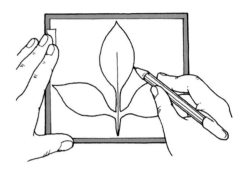

4 **To make a leaf**, trace the rose leaf B template from page 117 and transfer it onto one rectangle of mocha-brown handmade paper. Using the scissors, cut out the leaf.

5 Glue a length of florists' wire onto the leaf. Tape around the base of the leaf. To finish, continue taping to the end of the wire. Make a further three leaves.

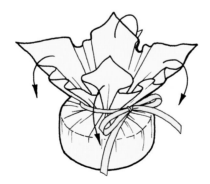

6 **To assemble the bouquet**, wrap the oasis foam in the gold gift wrap, arranging the folds into a ruffle. Place the beige organza ribbon loosely around the ruffle and tie its ends together in a bow. Open out the ruffle from the top, softly draping it over the oasis foam, as shown.

7 Arrange the leaves in the oasis foam so that they are in a square figuration. Softly bend them over towards the draped ruffle. To finish, arrange the roses and buds in the oasis foam. There are no hard and fast rules – flower arranging depends on personal taste and preference.

Modular Folding

Few things show paper's intrinsic beauty as well as folding multi-piece creations. Folding each piece and then joining the units with the completed project in mind is an enjoyable process. No intricate methods are involved; creating and joining the units is simple and easy. Modular folding does however take time, plenty of paper and a little patience and perseverance. Naturally, changing the colour or pattern of paper used can add still more variety to the designs. The first historical evidence for a modular origami design comes from a Japanese book by Hayato Ohoka published in 1734 called *Ranma Zushiki*. It contains a print called Origata, or fold models, which shows a group of traditional paper folds one of which is a modular cube.

Easy Unit-fold Coaster

The following model is based around a very easy unit-fold. Try making this in several different colours to vary its finished appearance, and to give you plenty of practice before you move on to the projects.

you will need

Two 21cm (8¼in) squares of origami paper in contrasting colours

Basic tool kit

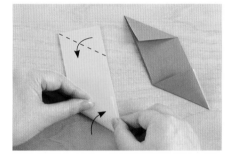

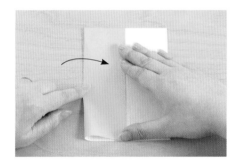

1 **To make one unit**, valley fold the left-hand side of one square of origami paper over to a point one-third of the way to the right, with the white side on top.

2 Valley fold the right-hand side over to the left so that it lies on top.

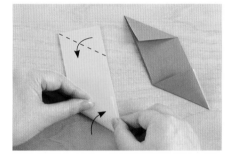

3 To finish, valley fold the top edge down to lie along the left-hand side and the bottom edge up to lie along the right-hand side. Repeat steps 1–3 with the remaining square of origami paper.

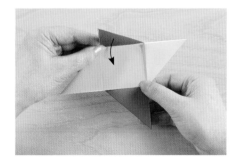

4 Place the units together crossways, as shown. Valley fold the top point down.

5 Valley fold the left-hand point over to the right and the bottom point up.

6 To finish, valley fold the right-hand point over to the left, while at the same time tucking it underneath the adjacent point so locking the units together.

Framed in Folds

The units in the following projects are based on a traditional origami windmill base, from which an indefinite number of forms can be created. A photo frame is a wonderful way of displaying your children's photographs, or memories of a much-loved pet, instead of having them hidden away in an old and dusty album. The photo wallet makes a delightful alternative to store valued mementos. Make its interior as decorative as possible and freely mix other treasured souvenirs in with your photographs. Finally, the photo cube is designed to show off four of your favourite photographs at once, and doubles as a handy pen or pencil holder.

Photo frame

you will need

18cm (7in) square of lavender striped paper

Two 6cm (2³⁄₈in) squares of purple craft card

8.5cm (3³⁄₈in) square photograph

Craft bow

Crystal glitter glue

Basic tool kit

Photo wallet

This fun design for a wallet allows you to keep three of your favourite photographs with you wherever you go. It is best to choose three images on the same theme, such as favourite pets or cherished vehicles. See page 98 for project instructions.

Finished size of photo frame: 9 x 9cm (3½ x 3½in)
Finished size of photo wallet: 9 x 31.5cm (3½ x 12³⁄₈in)
Finished size of photo cube: 9 x 9 x 9cm (3½ x 3½ x 3½in)

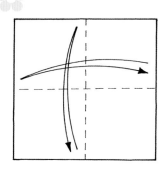

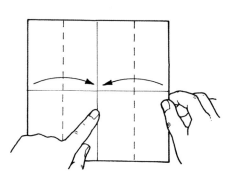

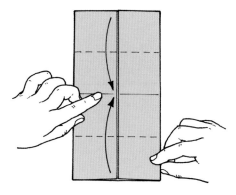

1 **To make a frame**, fold and unfold the square of lavender striped paper in half from side to side and top to bottom, with the white side on top.

2 Valley fold the sides in to the middle.

3 Valley fold the top and bottom edges in to the middle.

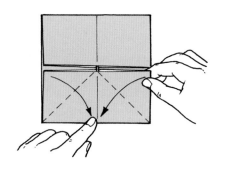

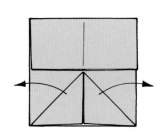

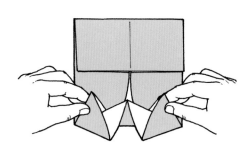

4 Valley fold the two side points of the lower flap down to meet the bottom edge.

5 Pinch the middle points and pull …

6 … their outer layers apart …

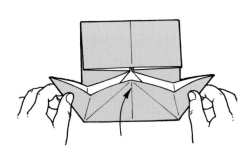

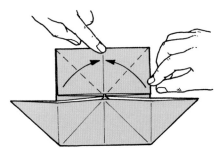

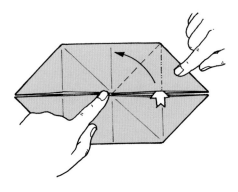

7 … flattening them out into a boat-like shape.

8 Valley fold the two side points of the upper flap up to meet the top edge. Repeat steps 5–7, making a windmill base.

9 Open out one triangular point and …

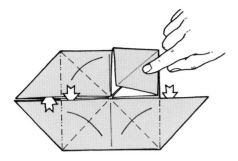

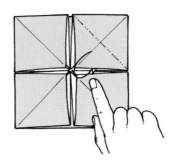

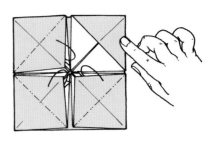

10 ... press it down neatly so that its tip meets the middle and makes a small square. Repeat steps 9 and 10 with the remaining three triangular points.

11 Mountain fold the front flap of one small square in half from the middle to the adjacent corner, making a corner pocket.

12 Repeat step 11 with the remaining three small squares. This completes the frame.

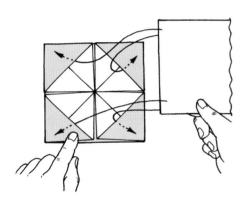

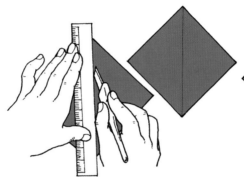

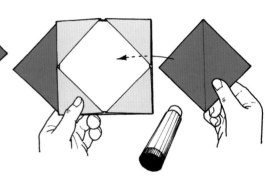

13 Tuck the corners of your photograph into the frame's four corner pockets, as shown.

14 Turn the squares of purple craft card around to look like diamonds. Lightly score them in half from top to bottom, making joining tabs.

15 Insert the joining tabs into the sides of the frame, as shown. Glue them firmly in place.

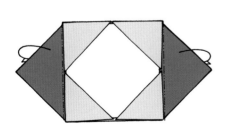

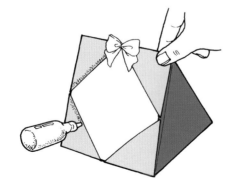

16 Along their scored lines, mountain fold each tab so that the frame can be made to stand up.

17 Apply a line of crystal glitter glue around the edges of the corner pockets. To finish, attach the craft bow to the frame, slightly below the middle point of its top edge, as shown.

Photo wallet

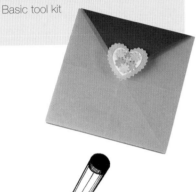

you will need

Three 18cm (7in) squares of paper
– one in light blue and two in blue

Three 6cm (2³/₈in) squares of blue
craft card

Three 8.5cm (3³/₈in) square
photographs

Small flower stickers

Sticky hook and loop pad

Heart craft sticker

Basic tool kit

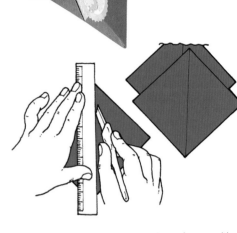

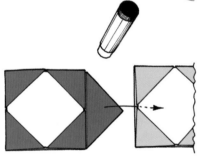

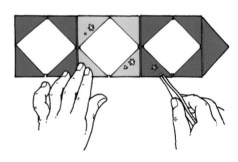

1 **To make the wallet**, begin by repeating steps 1–13 of the photo frame with the squares of light blue and blue paper and photographs.

2 Repeat step 14 of the photo frame with the squares of blue craft card.

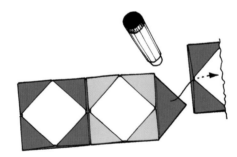

3 Insert one joining tab into the right-hand side of one blue frame and the left-hand side of the light blue frame. Glue it firmly in place.

4 Repeat step 3 with another tab and remaining blue frame, as shown.

5 Insert the remaining tab into the blue frame's right-hand side. Glue it firmly in place. Complete the decorations with small flower stickers.

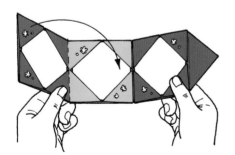

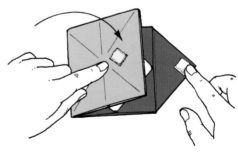

6 Along the scored lines of their joining tabs, valley fold the frames over and over from left to right.

7 Attach the sticky hook to the uppermost frame and the loop pad to the right-hand tab, as shown.

8 Along the scored line, valley fold the right-hand tab over, pressing the sticky hook and pad together. To finish, place the heart craft sticker on top of the frames, as shown.

Photo cube

you will need

Four 18cm (7in) squares
of pink marble paper

Four 6cm (2³/₈in) squares
of mocha-brown
craft card (small)

12.5cm (5in) square of mocha-
brown craft card (large)

Four 8.5cm (3³/₈in) square
photographs

Craft bow

Embellishments such as Christening
shoes, teddy bears and beach balls

Basic tool kit

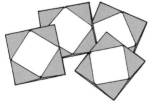

1 **To make the photo cube,** begin by repeating steps 1–13 of the photo frame with the squares of pink marble paper and photographs.

2 Repeat step 14 of the photo frame with the small squares of mocha-brown craft card.

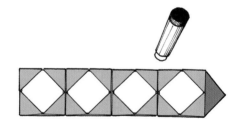

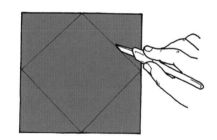

3 Insert the tabs into the sides of the frames, as shown. Glue them firmly in place.

4 Trace the photo cube base template from page 116 and transfer it onto the large square of mocha-brown craft card. Lightly score along the base's dashed lines.

5 Along their scored lines, valley fold the base's corners to stand vertically, making joining tabs.

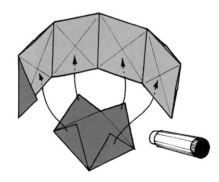

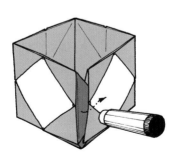

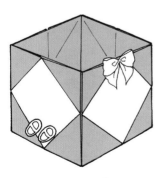

6 Turn the frames over and bring their two ends together, making a tube. Insert the base's tabs into the frames' lower pockets, as shown. Glue them firmly in place.

7 Carefully insert the remaining tab into the side of the adjacent frame. Glue it firmly in place.

8 To finish, complete the decorations with craft stickers and embellishments.

Nesting Boxes

This charming fold makes an ideal container for all sorts of small items, such as postage stamps and paper clips. A large colourful box is a novel way to present that special gift. Make a series of square boxes in graduating sizes and insert one inside the other, rather like a set of Russian dolls. They can be the same colour or different colours depending upon your personal preference. Or stack them together and use paper in primary colours to make a set with different coloured bases and lids. A 15cm (6in) square of origami paper or duo paper is perfect for smaller boxes. For an impressive looking gift box, use papers such as washi, vellum or gift wrap (see pages 6–7).

Rainbow of boxes

you will need

Two 20cm (8in) squares of red origami paper

Two 19cm (7½in) squares of orange origami paper

Two 18cm (7in) squares of warm yellow origami paper

Two 17cm (6¾in) squares of bright yellow origami paper

Two 16cm (6¼in) squares of lime green origami paper

Two 15cm (6in) squares of dark green origami paper

Two 14cm (5½in) squares of turquoise origami paper

Two 13cm (5¹/₈in) squares of light blue origami paper

Two 12cm (4¾in) squares of dark blue origami paper

Two 11cm (4⁵/₁₆in) squares of purple origami paper

Basic tool kit

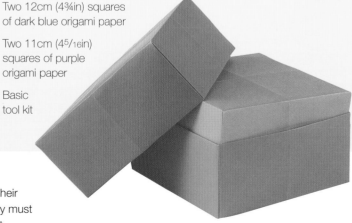

To enable the boxes to be nested inside each another their squares should reduce in size by about 1cm (³/₈in). They must be cut and folded very accurately for a successful result.
Finished size of boxes
Largest: 7.5 x 7.5 x 3.5cm (3 x 3 x 1⅜in)
Smallest: 4 x 4 x 2cm (1½ x 1½ x ¾in)

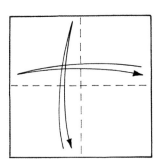

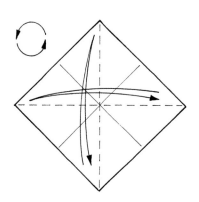

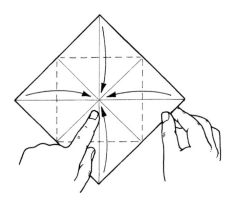

1 **To make the base**, fold and unfold the base's square of paper in half from side to side and top to bottom, with the white side on top.

2 Turn the square around to like a diamond. Valley fold the opposite corners together in turn to mark the diagonal fold-lines, then open up again.

3 Valley fold the corners in to the middle. Press them flat, making a blintz base.

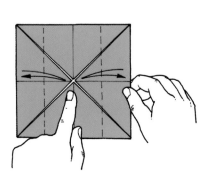

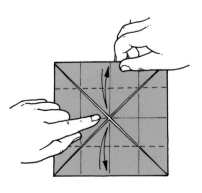

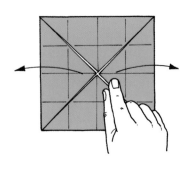

4 Valley fold the sides in to the middle. Press flat and unfold them.

5 Valley fold the top and bottom edges in to the middle. Press flat and unfold them.

6 Unfold the two middle corners, as shown.

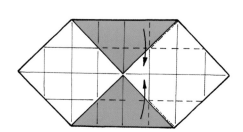

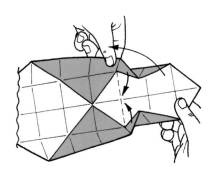

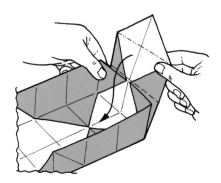

7 Using the existing valley and mountain fold-lines …

8 … form the right-hand side of the base.

9 Once again using the existing valley and mountain fold-lines, fold the side in to the base, thereby locking all the folds together.

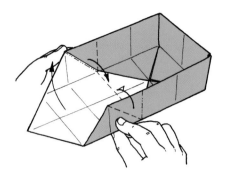

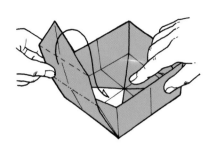

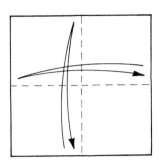

10 Repeat steps 7 and 8 at the opposite end of the paper, to form the base's left-hand side.

11 To complete, repeat step 9.

12 **To make the lid**, begin by repeating steps 1–3 of the base with the lid's square of paper.

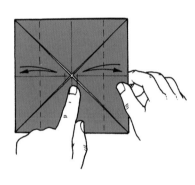

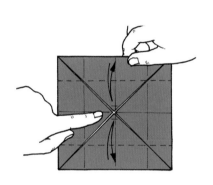

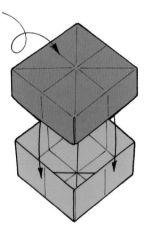

13 Valley fold the sides over to lie approximately 0.3cm (1/8in) short of the middle, as shown. Press flat and unfold them.

14 Valley fold the top and bottom edges over to lie approximately 0.3cm (1/8in) short of the middle, as shown. Press flat and unfold them. Repeat steps 6–11 of the base.

15 To finish, turn the lid over and slip it over the base.

Friends' gift boxes

These boxes have been made with male and female friends in mind. For the male box (gold), a 24cm (9½in) square of black paper was used for the base, and a 24cm (9½in) square of black and gold marble paper for the lid. For the female box (blue) a 21cm (8¼in) square of blue paper was used for the base, and a 21cm (8¼in) square of blue and glitter patterned paper was used for the lid. If a heavy gift is to be placed inside, it is advisable to glue a square of colour-coordinating craft card to the base of the box for reinforcement.

Quilt Folds

Everyone who has been fascinated by origami will revel in quilt folding, which is a style of folding paper so that it fits together to make another object. Quilt folding will inspire you to take on the challenge of creating your own models, transforming squares of paper into original accessories. One of the most exciting features of quilt folds is the overall impact of colour that the completed designs yield. With just a few small changes in the folding, it is very easy to produce new patterns and designs, including two different designs of coasters, a colourful pomander and a stunning rainbow-effect paper tapestry, each building in complexity. This technique was first introduced to us by Toshie Takahama.

Round coaster

you will need

20cm (8in) square of duo paper

Sticky-backed gem

Basic tool kit

Square coasters
The square coaster uses a different fold to the round coaster to create the cross pattern at the centre. See page 108 for project instructions. Both coasters are highly decorative and will add a truly personal touch to any table setting.
Finished size of round coasters: 10.5 x 10.5cm (4⅛ x 4⅛in)
Finished size of square coasters: 10 x 10cm (4 x 4in)

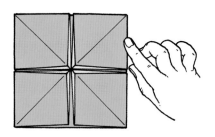

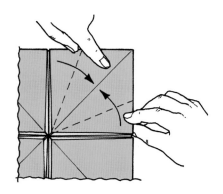

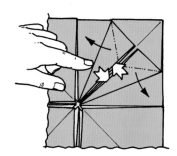

1 **To make a round coaster**, begin by repeating steps 1–10 for the photo frame on pages 96–97 with the square of duo paper, but with the colour required for the inside of the coaster on top in step 1.

2 Valley fold the inner two edges of one small square over so that they lie along the adjacent diagonal fold-line, as shown.

3 Open out one inner edge and press it down neatly in a diamond shape.

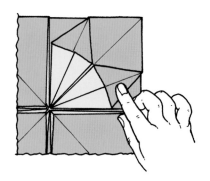

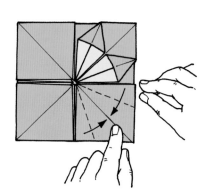

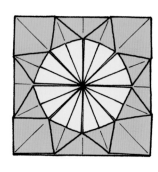

4 Repeat step 3 with the adjacent inner edge.

5 Repeat steps 2–4 with another small square.

6 Repeat steps 2–4 with the remaining two small squares.

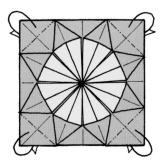

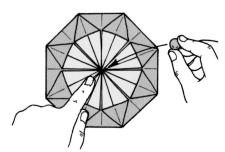

7 Mountain fold the four corners behind on a line that joins the tops of their respective inner edges, making triangular flaps on the reverse side.

8 To finish, place the sticky-backed gem in to the coaster's centre.

Pomander

you will need

Six 15cm (6in) squares of duo paper

Six sticky-backed gems

40cm (15¾in) length of 0.8cm (⁵/₁₆in) wide multi-coloured striped ribbon

Gold string

Basic tool kit

Hand-folded decorations such as this colourful pomander will be a welcome addition to any celebration; it will also add that all-important, personal touch. There are so many beautiful papers and ribbons to choose from today that no two pomanders will need to look alike.

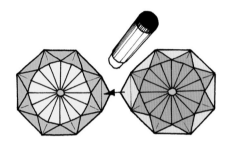

1 **To make a pomander**, begin by repeating steps 1–8 for the round coaster with the six squares of duo paper and sticky-backed gems. Unfold the coasters' triangular flaps. Glue two coasters together at their flaps, as shown.

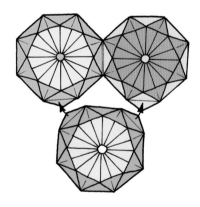

2 Glue another coaster into place so completing one half of the pomander.

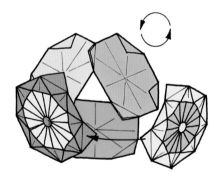

3 Glue the remaining coasters into place, forming a ball-like shape.

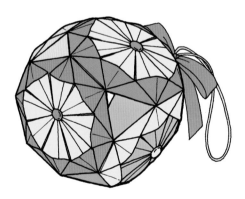

4 To finish, weave the ribbon through two of the pomander's triangular windows and tie its ends together in a bow. You can use the pomander by itself as a decoration, or hang it in a window by attaching a length of gold string and tying its ends together in a knot.

Square coaster

you will need

20cm (8in) square of duo paper

Sticky-backed gem

Basic tool kit

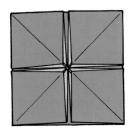

1 **To make a square coaster**, begin by repeating steps 1–10 for the photo frame on pages 96–97 with the square of duo paper, but with the colour required for the inside of the coaster on top in step 1.

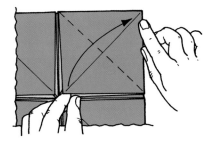

2 Valley fold the front flap of one small square in half from the middle to the adjacent corner.

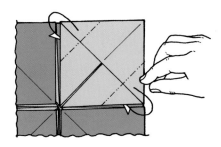

3 Mountain fold the small square's side points behind in to its middle, so tucking …

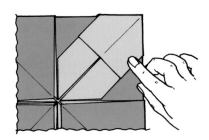

4 … them underneath the small square.

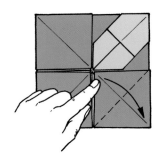

5 Repeat steps 2–4 with the remaining three small squares.

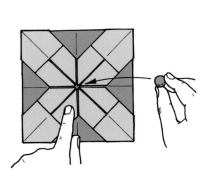

6 To finish, place the sticky-backed gem in to the coaster's centre.

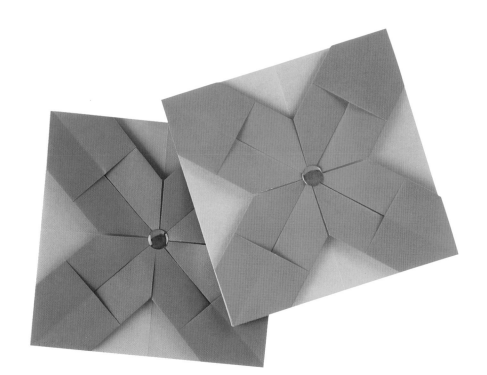

Quilt tapestry

Add an element of colour to your home with this appealing fold. To best complement the lines of the unit, avoid papers with heavy patterns, choosing simple or solid-coloured ones instead. For a clever alternative to a cloth tablemat, try this origami-inspired fold. It may take you a little time to make, but the creative effect it brings to your table is worth the effort. You'll find it more fun if you and a few friends can make this together.

Finished size of tapestry:
27cm (10½in) square
(approx)

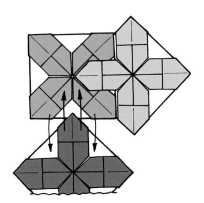

1 **To make a quilt tapestry,** begin by repeating steps 1–5 for the square coaster with the required number of squares of origami paper, but with the coloured side on top in step 1. Place one coaster on top of another, interlocking them, as shown. Glue them firmly together.

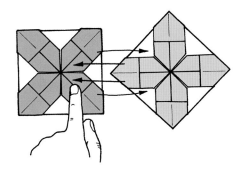

2 Interlock another coaster in place at the bottom and secure with a little glue.

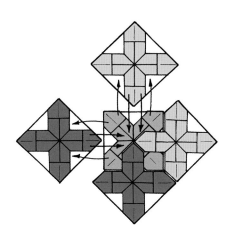

3 Interlock and glue two more coasters around the central structure, so making a block of coasters.

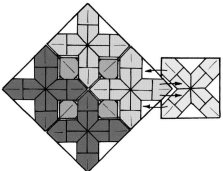

4 Place the block of coasters on top of a single coaster, interlocking them, as shown. Glue them firmly together. Continue building up blocks of coasters until you are satisfied with the tapestry's overall appearance. You can use the same coloured coasters each time a block is repeated in your tapestry, or you could try varying the colours in each block to make your tapestry look more visually complex.

Pinwheel Folds

The art of wrapping and the art of giving could be said to be one and the same. A beautifully presented gift shows that you have chosen and wrapped it with care. The pinwheel fold is easy to make and can look extremely decorative. Once you have mastered the basic method, many variations are possible. Often soft and light gifts require a delicate yet strong form of packaging, such as a decorative gift bag. The anticipation of an unopened gift bag has a special thrill of its own – its intriguing folds concealing the contents from the recipient. A disguising wrapping can add to the enthusiasm to reveal the contents.

Pinwheel gift bag

you will need

Twenty-four 15cm (6in) squares of pastel coloured origami paper

Two 5 x 30cm (2 x 12in) rectangles of heavyweight light blue paper

49 x 63cm (19¼ x 24¾in) rectangle of cream craft card

Basic tool kit

Pinwheel gift tag
Pinwheel-folded gift tags, made from one simple pinwheel unit, can make any gift more special. They can be attached with ribbon or glued directly onto the gift. The hole for the gift tie was punched using a regular office hole punch.
Finished size of gift bag: 31 x 21 x 7cm (12⅛ x 8¼ x 2¾in)
Finished size of gift tags: 7 x 7cm (2¾ x 2¾in)

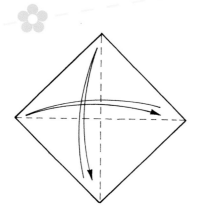

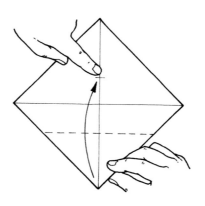

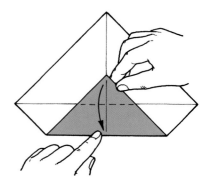

1 **To make a pinwheel fold**, turn one square of pastel origami paper around to look like a diamond, with the white side on top. Valley fold the opposite corners together in turn to mark the diagonal fold-lines, then open up again.

2 Valley fold the bottom corner up to a point one-third of the way to the top corner.

3 Valley fold the corner's tip down to meet the bottom edge.

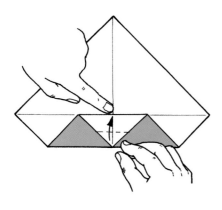

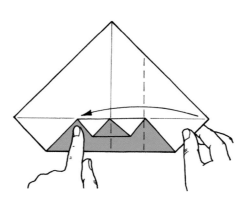

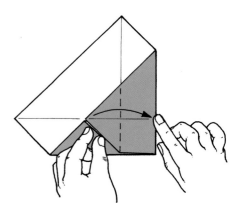

4 Valley fold the tip over to meet the intersection of the diagonal fold-lines.

5 Valley fold the right-hand corner over as far as shown.

6 Valley fold the corner's tip over to meet the right-hand side. Repeat step 4 with the tip.

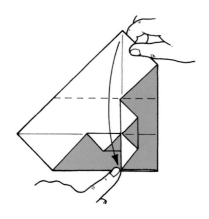

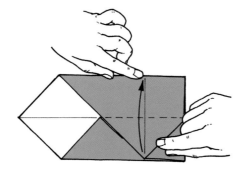

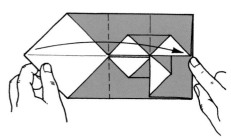

7 Valley fold the top corner down to meet the bottom edge.

8 Valley fold the corner's tip up to meet the top edge. Repeat step 4 with the tip.

9 Valley fold the left-hand corner over to meet the right-hand side.

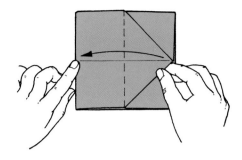

10 Valley fold the corner's tip over to meet the left-hand side. Repeat step 4 with the tip.

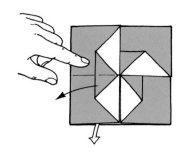

11 Lift up the left-hand flap of paper and open out the bottom flap of paper slightly.

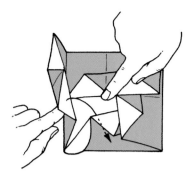

12 Refold the left-hand flap over along the existing vertical fold-line, while at the same time tucking its …

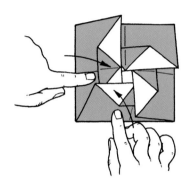

13 … lower half underneath the bottom flap of paper, as shown. To finish, press the paper flat. Make a further twenty-three pinwheel folds.

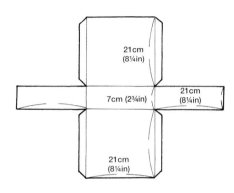

14 **To make the gift bag,** mark and measure out the illustrated gift bag template onto the cream craft card while making sure that the four joining tabs are no less than 1cm (³/₈in) wide. Using the craft knife, cutting mat and metal ruler, cut out the gift bag. Lightly score the fold-lines in place, as shown.

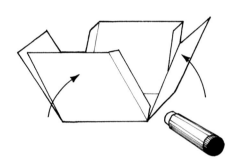

15 Along their scored lines, valley fold the bag's joining tabs, front and back surfaces and sides to stand vertically. Glue each tab to its adjacent side and press firmly in place.

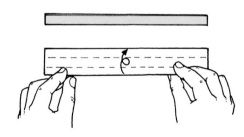

16 **To make the handles,** place one rectangle of light blue paper sideways on, with the white side on top. Divide the paper into three across its width by valley folding the bottom edge over and over, as shown. Repeat with the remaining rectangle.

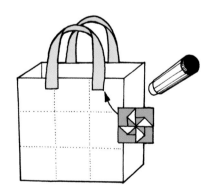

17 **To assemble,** glue the handles to the top of the bag, as shown. Neatly glue nine pinwheel folds, in a 3 x 3 grid, to the bag's front surface. Repeat on the back.

18 To finish, glue three pinwheel folds, in a vertical line, to each of the bag's sides.

Templates and Folding Patterns

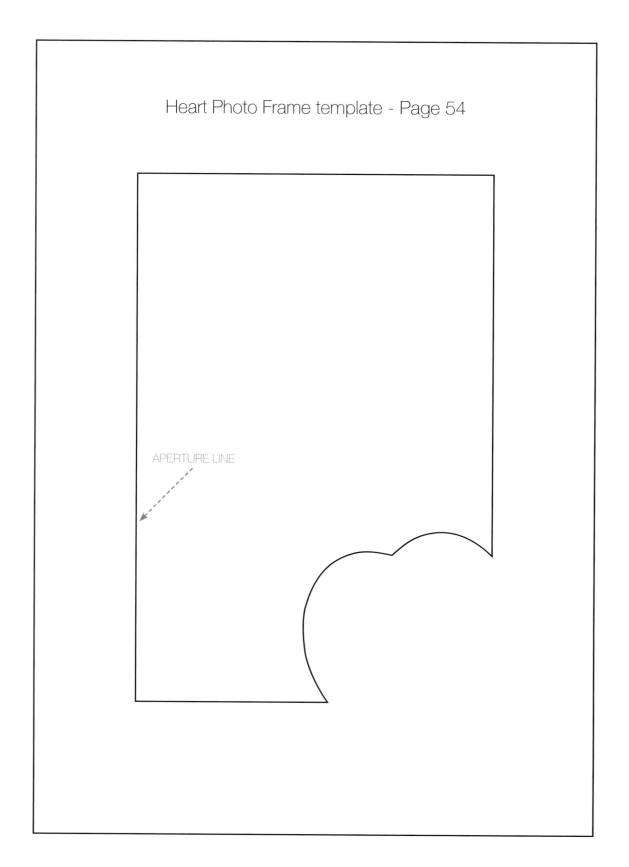

Heart Photo Frame template - Page 54

APERTURE LINE

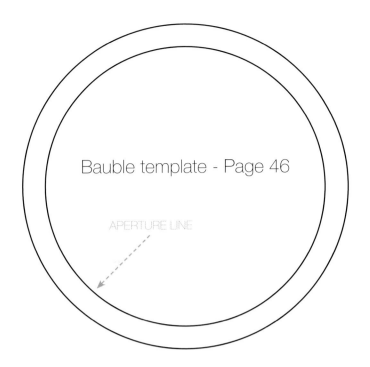

Bauble template - Page 46

APERTURE LINE

Bauble mat template - Page 46

Bauble folding pattern - Page 46

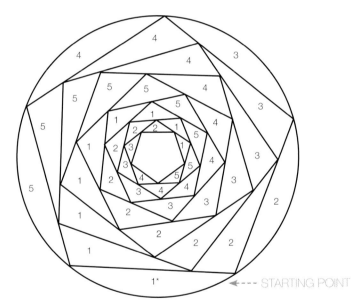

STARTING POINT

Heart template - Page 50

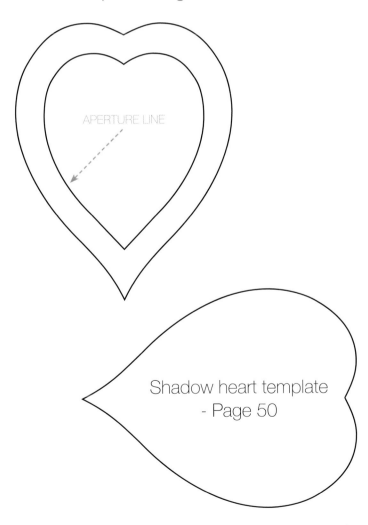

APERTURE LINE

Heart folding pattern - Page 50

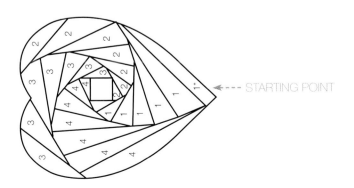

STARTING POINT

Shadow heart template
- Page 50

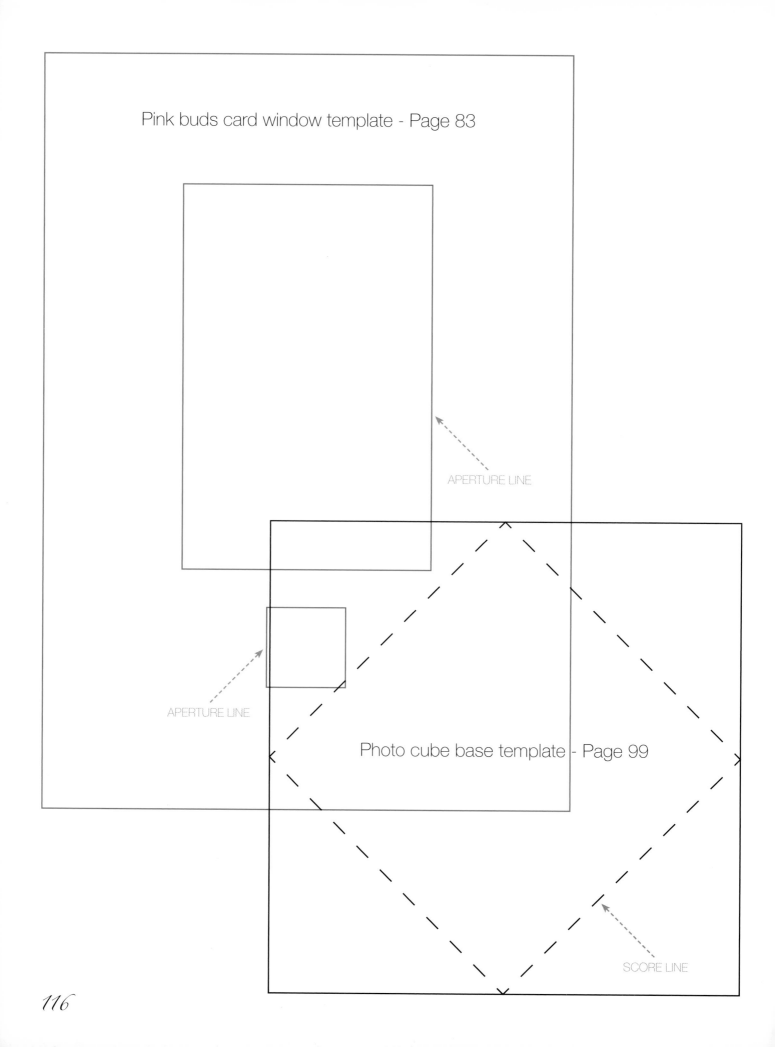

Pink buds card window template - Page 83

APERTURE LINE

APERTURE LINE

Photo cube base template - Page 99

SCORE LINE

Rose leaf A template - Page 88

Small buds card frame template - Page 80

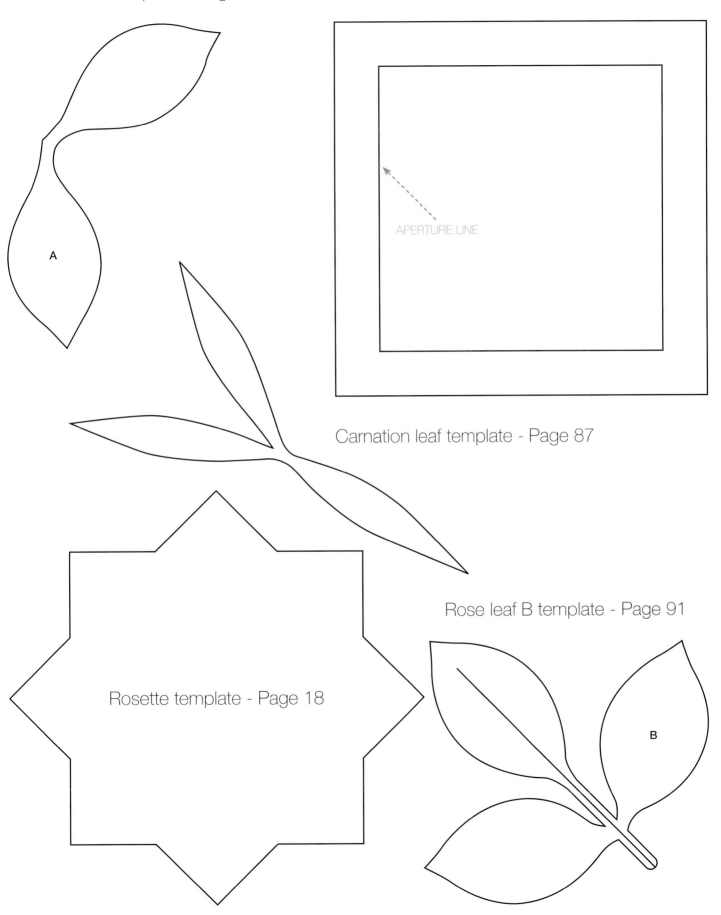

APERTURE LINE

A

Carnation leaf template - Page 87

Rose leaf B template - Page 91

Rosette template - Page 18

B

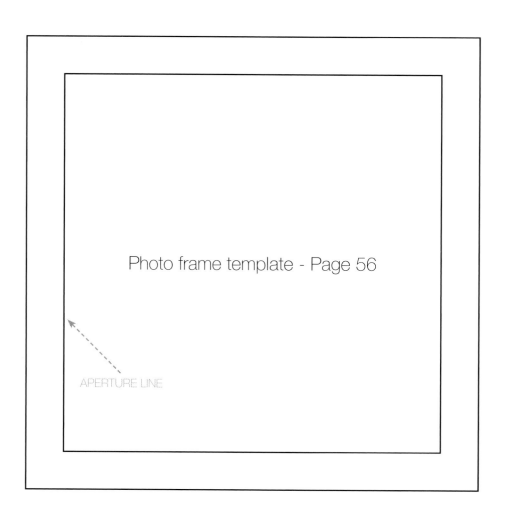

Photo frame template - Page 56

APERTURE LINE

Photo frame folding pattern - Page 56

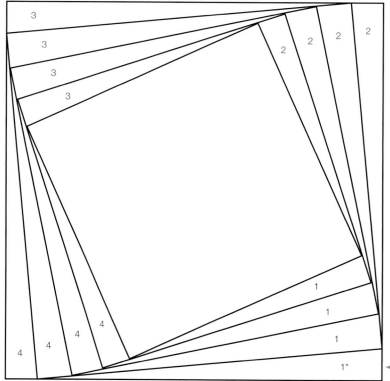

3
3
3
3

2
2
2
2

4
4
4
4
4

1
1
1
1*

◄--- STARTING POINT

Resources

The best approach for gathering the materials you require for paperfolding is to keep on the lookout and build up a stash gradually over time. Your local craft shop can order a particular product for you, give advice about materials and equipment and some shops may even offer regular craft clubs and workshops. The Internet gives access to a wider choice of suppliers from all over the world. Here are the details of a few suppliers to get you started.

United Kingdom

Creativity Cards and Crafts
5/6 The Labyrinth
7 Mark Lane
Eastbourne
East Sussex BN21 4RJ
tel/fax: 01323 439769
A craft shop and studio dedicated to paper crafts. Supplier of embellishments, peel-offs, tea bag and kaleidoscope papers and many other sundry items.

Falkiner Fine Papers
76 Southampton Row
London WC1B 4AR
tel: 020 7831 1151
email: falkiner@ic24.net
Handmade paper supplier. Mail-order service.

Japan Centre
212 Piccadilly
London W1J 9HG
tel: 020 7439 8035
fax: 020 7287 1082
email: info@japancentrebookshop.co.uk
www.japancentre.com
Origami and Japanese handmade paper supplier.

London Graphic Centre
16/18 Shelton Street
Covent Garden
London WC2H 9JL
tel: 020 7759 4500
fax: 020 7759 4585
www.londongraphics.co.uk
Stationery, graphic and fine art retailer.

Paperchase
Flagship Store and Main Office
213 Tottenham Court Road
London W1T 7PS
tel: 020 7467 6200
email: mailorder@paperchase.co.uk
www.paperchase.co.uk
Retailers of stationery, wrapping paper and art materials. Call for your nearest outlet.

Graphicus Limited
Fountain's Court
High Etherley
Bishop Auckland DL14 0LZ
tel: 01388 834934
www.graphicus.co.uk
Everything you need to make cards, embellishments, tools and equipment.

The Paper Warehouse
Grosvenor House Papers Ltd
Westmorland Business Park
Kendal LA9 6NP
tel: 01539 726161
email: info@ghpkendal.co.uk
www.ghpkendal.co.uk
General craft retailer of a wide range of paper craft supplies including punches and peel-offs.

Europe

Ideal Home Range
email: info@ihr-online.de
www.idealhomerange.com
Paper manufacturer. Contact for local stockists.

Kas Creative Wholesale
Industrieweg 27
Industrieterrein 'De Heuning'
Postbus 97
4050 EB Ochten
The Netherlands
tel: +31 (0) 344 642864
fax: +31 (0) 344 643509
email: info@kars.nl
www.kars.nl
Wholesaler of a vast range of craft materials. Contact for local stockists.

USA

Fascinating Folds
PO Box 10070
Glendale
AZ 85318
www.fascinating-folds.com
An extensive range of reference materials for paper art and crafts.

Nasco Arts and Crafts
4825 Stoddard Road
Modesto
CA 95397-3837
email: custer@eNASCO.com
www.nascofa.com
A comprehensive selection of art and craft materials.

Stamporium
1016 – 50th PL.W.
Mukilteo
WE 98275
www.stamporium.com
New and exciting paper-craft products imported from the Netherlands.

Twinrocker Handmade Paper
100 East 3rd Street
Brookston
IN 47923
www.twinrocker.com
Supplier of handmade paper and importer of decorative papers.

Australia

Glitzy Bits
www.glizybits.com.au
Online shop for handcrafted embellishments and punches.

Japanese Paper and Origami Supplies
PO Box 558
Summer Hill
NSW 2130
email: sales@origami.com.au
Supplier of Japanese handmade paper and origami products.

Scrap Booking Corner
PO Box 339
Helensburgh
NSW 2508
email: contactus@scrapbookingcorner.com.au
www.scrapbookingcorner.com.au
Stockist of stickers, papers, punches and deckle-edged scissors.

Paperfolding Societies

The following organizations offer a broad range of origami books, private publications on the various aspects of paperfolding, packaged origami paper and information on the many international origami associations. They also hold regular meetings and annual conventions that may include practical classes and exhibitions of the latest creations. They welcome folding enthusiasts of any age or level.

British Origami Society
The Membership Secretary
2A The Chestnuts
Countesthorpe
Leicestershire LE8 5TL
www.britishorigami.org.uk

The Envelope and Letterfold Association
PO Box 16181
London NW1
email: heide.karst@t-online.de

O.U.S.A. Centre of America
15 West 77th Street
New York
NY 10024-5192
www.origami-usa.org

The Australian Origami Society
www.freewebs.com/perthorigami

About the Authors

Steve Biddle is an author, entertainer and origami expert. He studied in Japan with the top Japanese origami masters where he acquired a deeper knowledge of a subject that had always fascinated him. He is also a member of the most famous magical society in the world, The Magic Circle, holding the degree of Associate of The Inner Magic Circle with Silver Star.

Megumi Biddle is a graphic artist, designer and illustrator with a long-standing interest in papercrafts and doll-making. At the 1985 All Japan Handcraft Art Society's exhibition, held in the Tokyo Art Museum, she received the society's top debut award for developing her own unique style of doll-making. She is also a highly skilled silhouette artist and has cut out the profiles of many well-known celebrities.

Steve and Megumi have presented their 'Paper Magic' act at a variety of functions and taken their act across the world, having performed in Europe, Australia, the United States and Japan. They have appeared on many television programmes, including *Blue Peter* and *The Generation Game* in the UK. Together, they have designed items for television, films and advertising campaigns and produced many highly successful craft and picture books both for children and adults. They live on the south coast of England with Hana, their Japanese Akita dog.

Acknowledgments

We would like to thank the following people: John Cunliffe for his technical support. For reviewing the text, Doreen and Caroline Montgomery. A special thank you to Rachael Brown and Sheena Tilley for testing the project instructions. For contributing photographs: Richard and Jayne Biddle, Ian and Donna Carter, and Tsuneo and Eriko Kimura. For allowing us to use their origami creations our deepest thanks go to the estates of: Toshio Chino for the Fantail Crane (page 76), Toshie Takahama for the Sports Shirt (page 32), Yacht (page 61) and Quilt Folds (page 104) and Michio Uchiyama for the Self-Closing Tato (page 40). Finally, we would like to express our gratitude to the David & Charles editorial and design teams.

Index

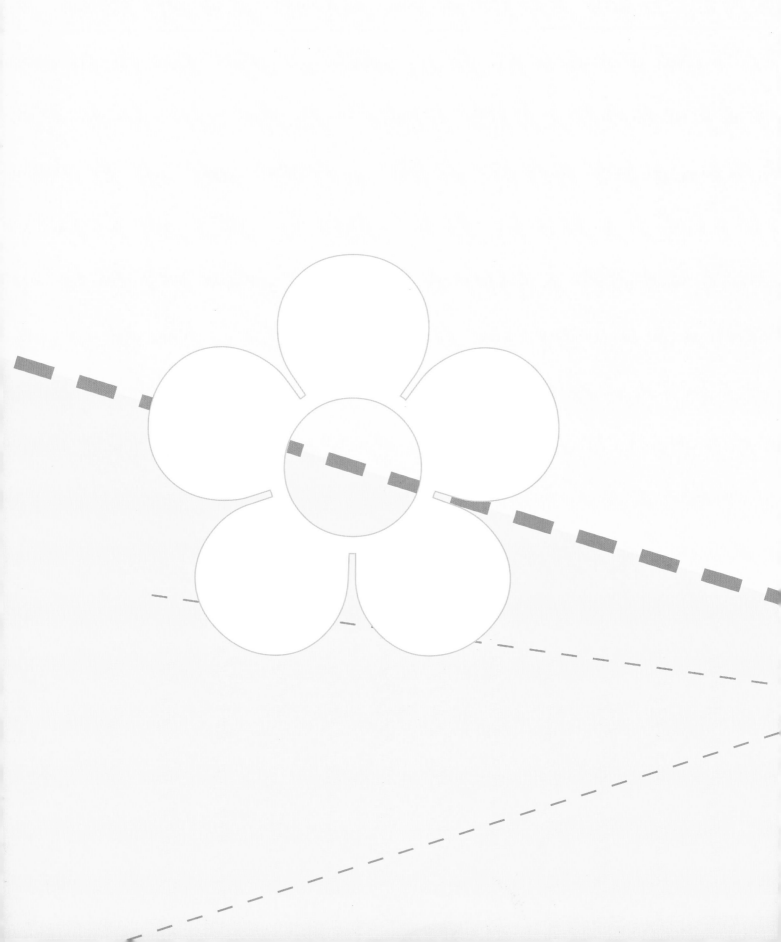